ROOTS AND LEGENDS

ROOTS
AND
LEGENDS

Folktales from African Culture

With Contributions by
KRISTIN G. CONGDON

wellfleet
press

CONTENTS

MORALS TAUGHT THROUGH ANIMAL TALES 69

BEARING WITNESS 121

PEOPLE WITH UNUSUAL POWERS 151

INTRODUCTION

Every culture has folktales. They were first communicated orally, then they were recorded. They are now rooted in our literature, songs, dances, visual art, and plays. Folktales communicate values, promote morals, and acknowledge experiences of oppression as a way to break free. They entertain while explaining why things are the way they are (even if they aren't) and use trickery to settle scores. While folktales have their roots in the past, they perform in and negotiate with the present.

This heirloom book of African legends (the term is used generically) is made up of multifaceted stories that have African cultural roots. Some reflect the reality of slavery and racism. They exist here as recorded history but they began as spoken storytelling due to the prominence of orality in Africa and the limited access that enslaved individuals had to the written word. Folktales gave levity to difficult lives as they provided hope for a better future. In Africa, and throughout the diaspora, folktales provided an otherworldly release that was socially sanctioned.

Telling tales became a way of confronting a powerful person without reprisal, such as an unpopular African chief or an enslaver. When these legends were told, laughter often followed, releasing pent up rage and displeasure. These folktales reorder the world around us as they focus on creating a better future by subverting power systems or describing a different version of our general understandings.

Thankfully, the legends in this book have survived due to folklorists, anthropologists, historians, and everyday people who shared them. They resonate today, still teaching important lessons and in some cases, offering comfort and a safe space for commiseration.

The creative content of these folktales allows animals to do everything people do. Many stories address the continual need to be fed and successfully grow crops. Some are about trickster animals who have less power than those who are physically stronger or who have more status. A character like Brer Rabbit may stand in for an enslaved person while another animal might represent the oppressor. This kind of coding was understood by enslaved individuals while plantation owners became outsiders, thinking the tales were harmless nonsense. Adapted to each new time and place, these tales cleverly reinvent the world. In nineteenth-century North Carolina, for example, Anansi tales became Ann Nancy stories. This was not only a change in gender but provided audiences with a name that was more comprehensible at the time. Folktales changed with each telling, morphing into expressions that functioned in new environments.

Shape-shifting is often used as a useful tool for escaping onerous situations or making something previously unthinkable materialize. Any person could temporarily become a spider, a fly, or an alligator, allowing for ease of mobility and a way to hide. Sometimes, shape-shifting was a technique used to spy on an adversary and gather information. Anansi, for example, successfully used his sharp-wittedness to overpower figures with more rank and reputation. For audiences, these legends provided power and might to those who needed it most. Telling stories was a means of bringing families and communities together as they generated hope and empowerment. Because the original tellers were far more connected to nature than we are today, their subjects often come from the mysteries of our natural world.

Cultural and geographical diversity define Africa. When Africans were kidnapped and forced to sail to the New World, they brought with them their connections to their homeland. African enslavement began in the Caribbean in the late sixteenth century and in colonial America in 1619, although there is a great deal of evidence that suggests the presence of slavery in what is now North America took place as early as the 1500s. While the importation of Africans for slavery was legally discouraged in 1808, Black immigration from Haiti brought refugees to the American mainland after the Haitian Revolution, and the British "United Empire Loyalists" (Tories) came to the eastern coast of the United States, bringing with them enslaved people.

Regardless of the 1808 legislation which made the

domestic sale of enslaved people in the United States illegal, both the American South and the North resisted, continuing their previous acts of brutal subjugation. In fact, the Northern maritime industry began to dominate the slave trade with the small state of Rhode Island controlling half of all the voyages in the United States. The former United States senator, James DeWolf, was potentially the largest slave trader in American history and members of the Brown family who were also involved in trafficking human beings gave considerable donations to Rhode Island College, which later became Brown University. The North not only imported Africans for slave trade and their own use, they sold them to individuals in the South and abroad. Folktales about slavery, therefore, continued into the Jim Crow era as our violent racial history carried on and was later remembered.

But African American folktales about slavery are neither solely a reaction to slavery or the adoption of African tales. Most scholars regard them as a creolization of the convergence of New World cultural traits, thereby resulting in a new form of storytelling. However, these tales also retain various Africanisms. Sometimes it can be difficult to determine which part of a folktale is African, especially considering Africa is comprised of fifty-four cultures.

The Creolization School, which came from the work of sociologists and folklorists in the early part of the twentieth century, maintained that African culture in the New World was a mixture of cultural thought. Africanisms could be found in dance, drama, speech patterns, foodways, hairstyles, music, family patterns, and folktales.

Although initially scholars disagreed on the way in which Africanisms were (or were not) maintained in the New World, in folktales, there are areas in which African American storytellers retained African motifs.

Melville Herskovits and W. E. B. Du Bois began groundbreaking work in this area by establishing the foundations for the Africanist School. They debunked the prevailing idea that African Americans dismantled their cultural identity because they came from fifty-four diverse cultures and were distributed in such a way that destroyed their culture of origin.

Robert Farris Thompson's work on what he called the existence of a "black Atlantic" tradition further established retention of African traditions, especially in dance, music, art, and philosophy. In African culture, for example, there is no detachment of an "art-for-art-sake" approach as there is in the West. One of Thompson's main organizing principles is the dominance of a percussive performance style, which has multiple meters and depends on a call and response in song but can take place in storytelling as well. Osanyin, the god of herbal medicine, coming mostly from the Kongo culture in Zaire and Angola, brought us the words "jazz" and "funky."

Among the African expressions that were retained and passed down through storytelling was spirit possession, demonstrated in what was called "The Frenzy," taken on by African priests and priestesses. The tradition of jumping the broom most likely came from West Africa and represents the separation of village life from untamed nature. The Kongo also gave us divination, the use of

graves as charms of ancestral observation, and the supernatural nature of trees. The root, High John the Conqueror, remains prevalent in today's American South, as does the decoration of graves with bottles and shells to honor the spirits of the dead.

The melding and retention of African folktales can also be seen with the African swindler, Brer Rabbit. Brer Rabbit is one of the most famous tricksters in all folktales, but especially in African American stories. However, Rabbit, as a fraudster, imposter, and charlatan can be found in stories from India, Europe, and in Buddhist folktales. Beatrix Potter's much-read tales about Peter Rabbit are rooted in stories told by Africans, although she did not give credit to her source. It was Joel Chandler Harris' *Uncle Remus: His Songs and His Sayings* (1880) and *Nights with Uncle Remus* (1883) that made them known to Americans.

In *Roots and Legends*, his stories from the 1907 collection, *Uncle Remus and Brer Rabbit*, are portrayed. They are told using African American vernacular English, thereby keeping a Black communication style that was then unfamiliar to white oppressors. Often referred to as Black folk speech or Black dialect, it is an Africanized English which expresses the conditions of enslavement while promoting a celebration of Black life and Black American folkways. While this is our main reason for including the Uncle Remus tales, it should be noted that the author, Harris, was a conservative white man writing mostly for white readers after the Civil War. The stories promoted the false idea that slavery was acceptable and competed with the historical truth. By telling these tales as he does, some conclude that what Harris is doing, as his shadow figure of Uncle Remus, is performing a minstrel show. Still, the tales are extremely popular, having been translated into over thirty languages and have had a significant influence on writers, both Black and white. But they can also be read as representative of how members of the human race treat each other with their ethnic differences, jealousies, and quarrelsome ways.

These tales express the need for power found through food, land, shelter, and other requirements for life. In order to survive, Brer Rabbit finds ways to overpower other animals, especially Wolf, who often represents enslavers or field bosses. As one legend informs another, there are similarities between Brer Rabbit stories and the John and Old Master tales. Both seek a one-upmanship and both look to owning more wealth and status.

The very survival of Africans in bondage, experiencing economic exploitation and political and social abuse, is grounded in the retention of their oral traditions, spoken like poetry and experienced as a sermon. As African Americans learned standard English, many maintained an ability to code-switch back to their folk speech, a melding of African and European-American languages. After whites associated it with a negative type of Black character, it began to be used in minstrel shows, produced and performed by whites to white audiences. Soon falling out of favor after World War I, an effort arose for the "new Negro" to take a more contemporary place in society, requiring what was called "mainstream American

English." According to the writer and civil rights activist James Weldon Johnson speaking artistically about Black dialect, "Negro dialect is naturally and by long association the exact instrument for voicing this phase of Negro life; and by that very exactness it is an instrument with but two full stops, humor and pathos." Today, creatives like Langston Hughes and Sterling K. Brown are praised for their form of Black speech which has been called "the genuine stuff," often coming from work songs and the blues. Black dialect should be seen as a blending of cultures and not as a debasement by a loftier culture.

From the white population's perspective, however, Africans in the United States were thought to have brought no culture with them because Africa was seen as uncivilized. If any aspects of the culture were discovered among the enslaved, it was attributed to Euro-American sources through copying. Because enslaved people were seen by whites as mentally weaker, they were assumed to have corrupted what they saw and heard. Yet when Black people's tales were considered rude or barbaric, Africa was credited as the source.

While trickster and shape-shifting tales are largely represented in this book, so too are stories of unmitigated physical strength, the quest for freedom, a peoples' poetic truth, and their unwavering creative spirit. The folktales shared here are rooted in African experiences, celebrate Black ancestry, and play an important role in our collective American and world histories. These stories have helped build a new and better world, supporting Black families by embracing and honoring their ancestry and heritage. The preservation of this folklore enables it to be enjoyed by generations to come, and today, the creativity of these tales continues to work its magic as it joyfully celebrates a proud African culture.

Kristin G. Congdon is Professor Emerita of Philosophy and Humanities at the University of Central Florida. She has published extensively on art, folklore, and multicultural education and in 2015, founded the Alliance for Truth and Justice, an all-volunteer group whose goal is to facilitate a new era of race relations through research, educational forums, exhibitions, and more.

WHY THINGS ARE THE WAY THEY ARE

This genre of African folklore teaches children about the world around them. Historically, this genre has helped Africans and African Americans ground themselves in a frequently hostile world. Traditionally told orally, these explanatory tales teach children about the nature of humanity, other creatures, the land surrounding them, the solar system, and beyond. A popular subsect of this genre is the fable, which explores the connection between animals and humans. Fables often explain specific elements of an animal's nature while also teaching lessons, as animals with human characteristics undergo entertaining and morally relevant trials and tribulations. Many of the tales in this broader genre have a significant moral element, demonstrating mistakes and deceptions that have caused specific elements of the world to arise. These tales present a unique and culturally significant way of processing the surrounding world, in which an unexpected event has a ripple effect that alters the nature of the universe.

Anansi and Nothing

Anansi, also spelled "Anancy" or "Annancy," is a shape-shifting spider who commonly takes the form of a human, mostly a man. He came to the New World with the enslaved Ashantis of West Africa. Known as a cunning trickster, he is much like the better-known Brer Rabbit, whose stories originated with the Yoruba and, in the New World, combined with tales from Native American and European traditions. Many folktales about Anansi explain how things came to be as we now know them. His tales, like this one, mostly depict him as having flawed character traits, such as his subjugation of women. There are often negative consequences to his bad behavior.

Near Anansi's miserable little hut there was a fine palace where lived a very rich man called Nothing. Nothing and Anansi proposed, one day, to go to the neighboring town to get some wives. Accordingly, they set off together.

Nothing, being a rich man, wore a very fine velvet cloth, while Anansi had a ragged cotton one. While they were on their way, Anansi persuaded Nothing to exchange clothes for a little while, promising to give back the fine velvet before they reached the town. He delayed doing this, however, first on one pretext, then on another—till they arrived at their destination.

Anansi, being dressed in such a fine garment, found no difficulty in getting as many wives as he wished. Poor

Nothing, with his ragged and miserable cloth, was treated with great contempt. At first, he could not get even one wife. At last, however, a woman took pity on him and gave him her daughter. The poor girl was laughed at very heartily by Anansi's wives for choosing such a beggar as Nothing appeared to be. She wisely took no notice of their scorn.

The party set off for home. When they reached the crossroads leading to their respective houses the women were astonished. The road leading to Anansi's house was only half cleared. The one which led to Nothing's palace was, of course, wide and well-made. Not only so, but his servants had strewn it with beautiful skins and carpets in preparation for his return. Servants were there, awaiting him, with fine clothes for himself and his wife. No one was waiting for Anansi.

Nothing's wife was queen over the whole district and had everything her heart could desire. Anansi's wives could not even get proper food; they had to live on unripe bananas with peppers. The wife of Nothing heard of her friends' miserable state and invited them to a great feast in her palace. They came and were so pleased with all they saw that they agreed to stay there. Accordingly, they refused to come back to Anansi's hut.

He was very angry, and tried in many ways to kill Nothing, but without success. Finally, however, he persuaded some rat friends to dig a deep tunnel in front of Nothing's door. When the hole was finished Anansi lined it with knives and broken bottles. He then smeared the steps of the palace with okra to make them very slippery and withdrew to a hiding spot.

When he thought Nothing's household was safely in bed and asleep, he called to Nothing to come out to the courtyard and see something. Nothing's wife, however, dissuaded him from going. Anansi tried again and again, and each time she bade her husband not to listen. At last, Nothing decided to go and see this thing. As he placed his foot on the first step he slipped, and down he fell into the hole. The noise alarmed the household. Lights were fetched and Nothing was found in the ditch, wounded so much by the knives that he soon died. His wife was terribly grieved at his untimely death. She boiled many yams, mashed them, and took a great many dishfuls of them round the district. To every child she met she gave some, so that the child might help her to cry for her husband. This is why, if you find a child crying and ask the cause, you will often be told he is "crying for nothing."

Why Spiders Are Always Found in the Corners of Ceilings

An Anansi tale is usually fun to read or listen to. Here, Anansi characteristically demonstrates his selfishness and insatiable appetite, as he deceives even his wife and son. His deceptions backfire as he gets stuck on a fake figure of a man. There are echoes of "Brer Rabbit and the Tar-Baby" in this folktale, which, in its original context, was a metaphor for a sticky state of affairs that gets worse once someone tangles with it.

❖ ❖ ❖

*E*gya Anansi was a very skillful farmer. He, with his wife and son, set to work one year to prepare a farm which was much larger than any they had previously worked. They planted it with yams, maize, and beans—and were rewarded by a very rich crop. Their harvest was ten times greater than any they had ever had before. Egya Anansi was very pleased when he saw his wealth of corn and beans.

He was, however, an exceedingly selfish and greedy man, who never liked to share anything—even with his own wife and son. When he saw that the crops were quite ripe, he thought of a plan whereby he alone would profit from them. He called his wife and son to him and spoke thus: "We have all three worked exceedingly hard to prepare these fields. They have well repaid us. Now that we have gathered in the harvest and packed it away in our barns, we are in need of a rest. I propose that you and our son should go back to our home in the village and remain there at your ease for two or three weeks. I have to go to the coast on very urgent business. When I return, we will all come to the farm and enjoy our well-earned feast."

Anansi's wife and son thought this a very good, sensible plan, and at once agreed to it. They went straight back to their village, leaving the cunning husband to start on his journey. Needless to say, he had not the slightest intention of doing so.

Instead, he built himself a very comfortable hut near the farm, supplied it with all manner of cooking utensils, gathered in a large store of the corn and vegetables from the barn, and prepared for a solitary feast. This went on for a fortnight. By that time Anansi's son began to think it was time for him to go and weed the farm, lest the weeds should grow too high. He accordingly went there and worked several hours on it. While passing the barn, he happened to look in. Great was his surprise to see that more than half of their magnificent harvest had gone. He was greatly disturbed, thinking robbers had been at work, and wondered how he could prevent further mischief.

Returning to the village, he told the people there what had happened, and they helped to make a rubber-man. When evening came, they carried the sticky figure to the farm, and placed it in the midst of the fields to frighten away the thieves. Some of the young men remained with Anansi's son to watch from one of the barns.

When all was dark, Egya Anansi (quite unaware of what had happened) came, as usual, out of his hiding place to fetch more food. On his way to the barn, he saw in front of him the figure of a man, and at first felt very frightened. Finding that the man did not move, however, he gained confidence and went up to him. "What do you want here?" said he. There was no answer. He repeated his question with the same result. Anansi then became very angry and dealt the figure a blow on the cheek with his right hand. Of course, his hand stuck fast to the rubber. "How dare you hold my hand?" he exclaimed. "Let me go at once or I shall hit you again." He then hit the figure with his left hand, which also stuck. He tried to disengage himself by pushing against it with his knees and body, until, finally, knees, body, hands, and head were all firmly attached to the rubber-man. There Egya Anansi had to stay till daybreak, when his son came out with the other villagers to catch the robber.

They were astonished to find that the evildoer was Anansi himself. He, on the other hand, was so ashamed to be caught in the act of greediness that he changed into a spider and took refuge in a dark corner of the ceiling lest anyone should see him. Since then, spiders have always been found in dark, dusty corners, where people are not likely to notice them.

How Wisdom Became the Property of the Human Race

In this Anansi tale, the trickster spider demonstrates his selfishness and vengeance while being outwitted by his son Kweku Tsin. Scholars of Caribbean culture assert that Anansi's weaknesses were created by colonialism which caused the enslaved to think creatively. Innovative and imaginative ways to deal with difficult situations were also practiced by many in the New World, especially during slavery. Anansi often uses deceit and deviousness as a way to survive.

◈ ◈ ◈

There once lived, in Fanti-land, a man named Father Anansi. He possessed all the wisdom in the world. People came to him daily for advice and help.

One day the men of the country were unfortunate enough to offend Father Anansi, who immediately resolved to punish them. After much thought he decided that the severest penalty he could inflict would be to hide all his wisdom from them. He set to work at once to gather again all that he had already given. When he had succeeded, he thought, in collecting it, he placed all in one great pot. This he carefully sealed, and determined to put it in a spot where no human being could reach it.

Now, Father Anansi had a son, whose name was Kweku Tsin. This boy began to suspect his father of some secret design, so he made up his mind to watch carefully. Next day he saw his father quietly slip out of the house, with his precious pot hung round his neck. Kweku Tsin followed. Father Anansi went through the forest till he had left the village far behind. Then, selecting the highest and most inaccessible-looking tree, he began to climb. The heavy pot, hanging in front of him, made his ascent almost impossible. Again and again he tried to reach the top of the tree, where he intended to hang the pot. There, he thought, wisdom would indeed be beyond the reach of every one but himself. He was unable, however, to carry out his desire. At each trial the pot swung in his way.

For some time Kweku Tsin watched his father's vain attempts. At last, unable to contain himself any longer, he cried out, "Father, why do you not hang the pot on your back? Then you could easily climb the tree."

Father Anansi turned and said, "I thought I had all the world's wisdom in this pot. But I find you possess more than I do. All my wisdom was insufficient to show me what to do, yet you have been able to tell me." In his anger he threw the pot down. It struck on a great rock and broke. The wisdom contained in it escaped and spread throughout the world.

Why the Lizard Continually Moves His Head Up and Down

This Anansi folktale is a fable, a common genre in African and African American storytelling. The origins of fables are unknown but they are especially popular with children who enjoy exploring fantasy through storytelling. Fables are generally about animals with human traits, denoting a strong connection between the natural world and humans. In this story, as in most fables, a lesson is taught or an explanation is given for distinguishing characteristics of an animal. While the story recognizes the lizard's gestures, scientists tell us its head movement is actually a way of communicating.

🔷 🔷 🔷

In a town not very far from Anansi's home lived a great king. This king had three beautiful daughters, whose names were kept a secret from everybody except their own family. One day their father made a proclamation that his three daughters would be given as wives to any man who could find out their names. Anansi made up his mind to do so.

He first bought a large jar of honey and set off for the bathing-place of the king's daughters. Arriving there, he climbed to the top of a tree which grew some very fine fruit. He picked some of this fruit and poured honey over it. When he saw the princesses approaching, he dropped the fruit on the ground and waited. The girls thought the fruit dropped of its own accord, and one of them ran forward to pick it up. When she tasted it, she called out to her sisters by name to exclaim at its sweetness. Anansi dropped another, which the second princess picked up— she, in her turn, called out the names of the other two. In this fashion Anansi found out all their names.

As soon as the princesses had gone Anansi came down from the tree and hurried into the town. He went to all the great men and summoned them to a meeting at the King's palace on the morrow.

He then visited his friend Lizard, to get him to act as herald at Court next day. He told Lizard the three names and that he was to sound them through his trumpet when the time came.

Early the next morning, the King and his court were assembled as usual. All the great men of the town appeared, as Anansi had requested. Anansi stated his business, reminding the King of his promise to give his three daughters to the man who had found out their names. The King demanded to hear the names, whereupon Lizard sounded them on his trumpet.

The King and courtiers were very surprised. His Majesty, however, could not break the promise he had made of giving his daughters to the man who named them. He accordingly gave them to Lizard. Anansi was very angry and explained that he had told the names to Lizard, so that meant he ought to get at least two of the girls, while Lizard could have the third. The King refused. Anansi then begged hard for even one, but that was also refused. He went home in a very bad temper, declaring that he would get revenge on Lizard for stealing his wives away.

He thought over the matter very carefully but could not find a way of punishing Lizard. At last, however, he had an idea.

He went to the King and explained that he was setting off next morning on a long journey. He wished to start very early, and so begged the King's help. The King had a fine rooster, which always crowed at daybreak to waken the King if he wished to get up early. Anansi begged that the King would command the rooster to crow next morning, so that Anansi would be sure to set off in time. This the King readily promised.

As soon as night fell Anansi went by a back way to the rooster's sleeping-place, seized the bird quickly, and killed it. He then carried it to Lizard's house, where all were in bed. There he quietly cooked the rooster, placed the feathers under Lizard's bed, and put some of the flesh on a dish close to Lizard's hand. The wicked Anansi then took some boiling water and poured it into poor Lizard's mouth, thus making him unable to speak.

When morning came, Anansi went to the King and reproached him for not letting the rooster crow. The King was much surprised to hear that it had not obeyed his commands.

He sent one of his servants to find and bring the rooster to him, but, of course, the servant returned empty-handed. The King then ordered them to find the thief. No trace of him could be found anywhere. Anansi then cunningly said to the King: "I know Lizard is a rogue, because he stole my three wives from me. Perhaps he is the thief?" Accordingly, the men went to search Lizard's house.

There, of course, they found the remnants of the rooster, cooked ready to eat, with its feathers under the bed. They questioned Lizard, but the poor animal was unable to reply. He could only move his head up and down helplessly. They thought he was refusing to speak, so they dragged him before the King. To the King's questions he could only return the same answer, and His Majesty got very angry. He did not know that Anansi had made Lizard unable to speak. Lizard tried very hard to speak, but in vain.

He was judged guilty of theft, and as a punishment, his wives were taken away from him and given to Anansi.

Since then, lizards have always had a way of moving their heads helplessly backward and forward, as if saying, "How can anyone be so foolish as to trust Anansi?"

Why We See Ants Carrying Bundles as Big as Themselves

In this story, Kweku Anansi and his son, Kweku Tsin, are faced with circumstances beyond their control when there is no rain for their crops. The answer to their dilemma, as is often true, can come from unexpected places. But when Anansi gets greedy and tries to figure out how to reap more rain than his son has for his fields, a series of calamities take place. In many stories about Anansi, such as this one, his flawed character traits have negative consequences. But being the trickster that he is, Anansi makes a plan involving Mr. Ant. Ultimately, we learn what trusting an unsavory character means for the ants we see today. But this tale also provides an explanation for the incredible strength that ants now have.

Kweku Anansi and Kweku Tsin—his son—were both very clever farmers. Generally, they succeeded in getting fine harvests from each of their farms. One year, however, they were very unfortunate. They had sown their seeds as usual, but no rain had fallen for more than a month after and it looked as if the seeds would be unable to sprout.

Kweku Tsin was walking sadly through his fields one day looking at the bare, dry ground, wondering what he and his family would do for food if they were unable to get any harvest. To his surprise he saw a tiny dwarf seated by the roadside. The little hunchback asked the reason for his sadness, and Kweku Tsin told him. The dwarf promised to help him by bringing rain to the farm. He bade Kweku Tsin fetch two small sticks and tap him lightly on the hump, while he sang:

"O water, go up, O water, go up,
And let rain fall, and let rain fall."

To Kweku Tsin's great joy rain immediately began to fall and continued until the ground was thoroughly soaked. In the following days the seeds germinated and the crops began to promise well.

Anansi soon heard how well Kweku Tsin's crops were growing—whilst his own fields were still bare and hard. He went straightway to his son and demanded to know the reason. Kweku Tsin, being an honest fellow, at once told him what had happened.

Anansi quickly made up his mind to get his farm watered in the same way, and accordingly set out toward it. As he went, he cut two big, strong sticks, thinking, "My son made the dwarf work with little sticks. I will make him do twice as much with my big ones." He carefully hid the big sticks, however, when he saw the dwarf coming toward him. As before, the hunchback asked what the trouble was, and Anansi told him. "Take two small sticks, and beat me lightly on the hump," said the dwarf. "I will get rain for you."

But Anansi took his big sticks and beat them so hard that the dwarf fell down dead. The greedy fellow was now thoroughly frightened, for he knew that the dwarf was jester to the King of the country, and a great favorite of His Majesty. He wondered how he could fix the blame on someone else. He picked up the dwarf's dead body and carried it to a kola-tree. There he laid it on one of the top branches and sat down under the tree to watch.

Kweku Tsin came along to see if his father had succeeded in getting rain for his crops. "Did you not see the dwarf, father?" he asked, as he saw the old man sitting alone. "Oh, yes!" replied Anansi, "but he has climbed this tree to pick kola. I am now waiting for him."

"I will go up and fetch him," said the young man—and immediately began to climb. As soon as his head touched the body it fell to the ground. "Oh! what have you done, you wicked fellow?" cried his father. "You have killed the King's jester!"

"That is all right," replied the son quietly (who saw that this was one of Anansi's tricks). "The King is very angry with him and has promised a bag of money to anyone who would kill him. I will now go and get the reward."

"No! No! No!" shouted Anansi. "The reward is mine. I killed him with two big sticks. I will take him to the King."

"Very well!" was the son's reply. "As you killed him, you may take him."

Off set Anansi, quite pleased with the prospect of getting a reward. He reached the King's court, only to find the King very angry at the death of his favorite jester. The body of the jester was shut up in a great box and Anansi was condemned to carry it on his head forever as punishment. The King enchanted the box so that it could never be set down on the ground. The only way in which Anansi could ever get rid of it was by getting some other man to put it on his head. This, of course, no one was willing to do.

At last, one day, when Anansi was almost worn out with his heavy burden, he met Ant. "Will you hold this box for me while I go to market and buy some things I need badly?" said Anansi to Mr. Ant.

"I know your tricks, Anansi," replied Ant. "You want to be rid of it."

"Oh, no, Mr. Ant," protested Anansi. "I will come back for it, I promise."

Mr. Ant, who was an honest fellow, and always kept his own promises, believed him. He took the box on his head, and Anansi hurried off. Needless to say, the sly fellow had not the least intention of keeping his word. Mr. Ant waited in vain for his return—and was obliged to wander all the rest of his life with the box on his head. That is the reason we so often see ants carrying great bundles as they hurry along.

Thunder and Anansi

*Many Anansi tales portray the quick-wittedness and
craftiness required for survival. Here, hungry Anansi
sees a palm tree on a small island and attempts to
feed himself by plucking palm nuts, which we think
of as the fruit of the tree. After that doesn't work, he
meets Thunder, who provides him with sustenance.
His downfall, however, is his constant selfishness.
Like Anansi, his son, Kweku Tsin, also has shape-
shifting powers which he uses to once again discover
his father's self-centered ways. Like Kweku Tsin,
Mrs. Anansi is more altruistic. But when she seeks
revenge for her husband's deceitfulness, her scheme
doesn't end well. When Anansi asks Thunder for help
once more, this second encounter results in a most
unfavorable outcome.*

There had been a long and severe famine in the land
where Anansi lived. He had been quite unable to
obtain food for his poor wife and family. One day, gazing
desperately out to sea, he saw, rising from the midst of the
water, a tiny island with a tall palm tree upon it. He was
determined to reach this tree—by any means possible—and
climb it, in the hope of finding a few nuts to reward him.
How to get there remained uncertain.

This, however, solved itself when he reached the beach,
for there lay the means to reach the island: an old broken

boat. It certainly did not look very strong, but Anansi decided to try it.

His first six attempts were unsuccessful—a great wave dashed him back on the beach each time he tried to put off. He was persevering, however, and the seventh trial was successful. He steered the battered old boat as best he could, and at length reached the palm tree he desired. Having tied the boat to the trunk of the tree—which grew almost straight out of the water—he climbed toward the nuts. Plucking all he could reach, he dropped them, one by one, down to the boat. To his dismay, every single one missed the boat and fell, instead, into the water, until only the last one remained. This he aimed even more carefully than the others, but it also fell into the water and disappeared from his hungry eyes. He had not tasted even one and now all were gone.

He could not bear the thought of going home empty-handed, so, in his despair, he threw himself into the water, too. To his complete astonishment, instead of being drowned, he found himself standing on the sea floor in front of a pretty, little cottage. From it emerged an old man, who asked Anansi what he wanted so badly that he had come to Thunder's cottage. Anansi told his tale of woe, and Thunder showed himself to be most sympathetic.

He went into the cottage and fetched a fine cooking pot, which he presented to Anansi, telling him that he need never be hungry again. The pot would always supply enough food for himself and his family. Anansi was most grateful, and left Thunder with many thanks.

Being anxious to test the pot at once, Anansi only waited till he was again seated in the old boat to say, "Pot,

pot, what you used to do for your master, do now for me."
Immediately good food of all sorts appeared. Anansi ate a
hearty meal, which he very much enjoyed.

On reaching land again, his first thought was to run home
and give all his family a good meal from his wonderful pot.
A selfish, greedy fear prevented him. "What if I should use
up all the magic of the pot on them and then have nothing
more left for myself!? Better keep the pot a secret—then I
can enjoy a meal when I want one." So, his mind full of this
thought, he hid the pot.

He reached home, pretending to be utterly worn out with
fatigue and hunger. There was not a grain of food to be had
anywhere. His wife and poor children were weak for want
of it, but selfish Anansi took no notice. He congratulated
himself at the thought of his magic pot, now safely hidden
in his room. There he retired from time to time when he
felt hungry and enjoyed a good meal. His family got
thinner and thinner, but he grew plumper and plumper.
They began to suspect Anansi held some secret and were
determined to find it out. His eldest son, Kweku Tsin, had
the power of changing himself into any shape he chose, so,
he took the form of a tiny fly and accompanied his father
everywhere. At last, Anansi, feeling hungry, entered his
room and closed the door. Next, he took the pot, and had
a fine meal. Having replaced the pot in its hiding place,
he went out, on the pretense of looking for food.

As soon as he was safely out of sight, Kweku Tsin
fetched out the pot and called all his hungry family to
come at once. They had as good a meal as their father
had had. When they had finished, Mrs. Anansi—to punish

her husband—said she would take the pot down to the
village and give everybody a meal. This she did—but alas,
in working to prepare so much food at one time, the pot
grew too hot and melted away. What was to be done now?
Anansi would be so angry! His wife forbade everyone to
mention the pot.

Anansi returned, ready for his supper, and, as usual,
went into his room, carefully shutting the door. He went
to the hiding place only to find it was empty! He looked
around in consternation. No pot was to be seen anywhere.
Someone must have discovered it. His family must be the
culprits; he would find a means to punish them.

Saying nothing to anyone about the matter, he waited
till morning. As soon as it was light, he started off towards
the shore, where the old boat lay. Getting into the boat, it
started of its own accord and glided swiftly over the water—
straight for the palm tree. Arriving there, Anansi attached
the boat as before and climbed the tree. This time, unlike
the last, the nuts almost fell into his hands. When he aimed
them at the boat they fell easily into it—not one dropping
into the water as before. He deliberately took them
from the boat and threw them overboard, immediately
jumping after them. As before, he found himself in front of
Thunder's cottage, with Thunder waiting to hear his tale.
This he told, the old man showing the same sympathy as
he had previously done.

This time, however, he presented Anansi with a fine stick
and bade him good-bye. Anansi could scarcely wait till he got
into the boat—so anxious was he to try the magic properties
of his new gift. "Stick, stick," he said, "what you used to do

for your master, do for me also." The stick began to beat him so severely that, in a few minutes, he was obliged to jump into the water and swim ashore, leaving the boat and stick to drift away where they pleased. Then he returned sorrowfully homeward, bemoaning his many bruises and wishing he had acted more wisely from the beginning.

Ohia and the Thieving Deer

In many folktales, there is a poor man or family and someone who graciously forms a partnership to provide them with assistance. In this case, it is a kind farmer who has palm trees which could produce palm wine. This alcoholic beverage, indigenous to the tropical regions of Africa, is produced by the spontaneous yeast-lactic fermentation of the sweet sap from the palm trees. When a couple's dream fails, Ohia and Awirehu begin to despair. But when Ohia sets out to discover why the wine continually goes missing, he encounters a deer, a group of quadrupeds (four-legged animals), and eventually King Tiger. Because of his hardships Ohia receives a great gift that he promises to keep secret. Unfortunately, sometimes a promise is very hard to keep, especially when greater riches are possible.

There once lived upon the earth a poor man called Ohia, whose wife was named Awirehu. This unfortunate couple had suffered one trouble after another. No matter what they took in hand, misfortune seemed to lie in wait for them. Nothing they did met with success. They became so poor that eventually they could scarcely obtain cloth with which to cover themselves.

Finally, Ohia thought of a plan which many of his neighbors had tried and found successful. He went to a wealthy farmer who lived nearby and offered to hew down several of his palm trees. He would then collect their sap to make palm wine. When this should be ready for the market, his wife would carry it there and sell it. The proceeds would then be divided equally between the farmer, Ohia, and Awirehu.

This proposal was laid before the farmer and he was quite willing to agree to it. Not only so, but he granted Ohia a supply of earthen pots in which to collect the sap, as the miserable man was far too poor to buy any.

In great delight, Ohia and his wife set to work. They cut down the trees and prepared them—setting the pots underneath to catch the sap. Before the rooster crowed on market day, Ohia set off with a lighted torch to collect the wine and prepare it for his wife to take into the town. She was almost ready to follow.

To his great distress, on arriving at the first tree, instead of finding his earthen pot filled with the sweet sap, he saw it lying in pieces on the ground—the wine all gone. He went on to the second and third trees—but there, and at all the others, too, the same thing had happened.

His wife, in high spirits and ready for the market, joined him at that moment. She saw at once by his face that some misfortune had again befallen them. Sorrowfully, they examined the mischief, and agreed that some wicked person had stolen the wine and then broken the pots to hide the theft. Awirehu returned home in despair, but Ohia set to work once more. He fetched a second batch of pots from what was left over from the farmer's first supply and placed them all ready to catch the sap.

On his return to the trees the next morning, he found that the same behavior had been repeated. All his wine was again stolen and his pots in fragments. He had no other option but to go to the farmer and tell him of these fresh misfortunes. The farmer proved to be very kind and generous and gave orders that Ohia might have as many pots as he should require.

Once more the poor fellow returned to the palm trees and set his pots ready. This third attempt, however, met with no better result than the two previous. Ohia went home in despair. His wife was of the opinion that they should give up trying to overcome their evil fortunes. It was quite evident that they could never attain success. The husband, however, determined that, at least, he would find and punish the culprit, if that were possible.

Accordingly, he bravely set his pots in order for the last time. When night came, he remained on guard among the trees. Midnight passed and nothing happened, but toward two o'clock in the morning, a dark form glided past him to the nearest palm tree. A moment later, he heard the sound of a breaking pot. He stole up to the form. On approaching it he found that the thief was a bush-deer, carrying on its head a large jar, into which it was pouring the wine from Ohia's pots. As it emptied them it threw them carelessly on the ground, breaking them into pieces.

Ohia ventured a little nearer, intending to seize the culprit. The bush-deer, however, was too quick for him and escaped, dropping his great pot on the ground as he ran. The deer was swift, but Ohia had fully determined to catch him, and so, followed. The chase continued over many miles until midday arrived, at which time they had reached the bottom of a high hill. The deer immediately began to climb, and Ohia—though almost tired out—still followed. Finally, the summit of the hill was reached, and there Ohia found himself in the midst of a great gathering of quadrupeds. The deer, panting, threw himself on the ground before King Tiger. His Majesty commanded that Ohia should be brought before him to be punished for this intrusion into such a serious meeting.

Ohia begged for a hearing before they condemned him. He wished to explain fully his presence there. King Tiger, after consulting with some of the other animals, agreed to listen to his tale. Thereupon Ohia began the story of his unfortunate life. He told how one trial after another had befallen him, and how, finally, he had thought of the palm wine. He described his feelings on discovering the first theft after all his labor. He related his second, third, and fourth attempts, with the result of each. He then went on to tell of his chase after the thief, and thus explained his presence at their conference.

The quadrupeds listened very attentively to the recital of Ohia's troubles. At the conclusion they unanimously agreed that the deer was the culprit and the man blameless. The former was accordingly sentenced to punishment, while the latter received an apology in the name of the entire conference. King Tiger, it appeared, had each morning given the deer a large sum of money wherewith to purchase palm wine for the whole assembly. The deer had stolen the wine and kept the money.

To make up to Ohia for his losses, King Tiger offered him, as a gift, the power of understanding the conversation of all animals. This, said he, would speedily make Ohia a rich man. But he attached one condition to the gift. Ohia must never—on pain of instant death—tell anyone about his wonderful power.

The poor man, much delighted, set off for home. When it was reached, he lost no time in setting to work at his palm trees again. From that day his troubles seemed to be over. His wine was never interfered with, and he and Awirehu became more and more prosperous and happy.

One morning, while he was bathing in a pool quite close to his house, he heard a hen and her chickens talking together in his garden. He listened, and distinctly heard a chicken tell Mother Hen about three jars of gold buried in Ohia's garden. The hen bade the chicken be careful, lest her master should see her scraping near the gold, and so discover it.

Ohia pretended to take no notice of what they were saying and went away. Presently, when Mother Hen and her brood had gone, he came back and commenced digging in that part of the garden. To his great joy, he soon found three large jars of gold. They contained enough money to keep him in comfort all his life. He was careful, however, not to mention his treasure to anyone but his wife. He hid it safely inside his house.

Soon he and Awirehu had become one of the richest couples in the neighborhood and owned quite a large amount of property. Ohia thought he could afford now to keep a second wife, so he married again. Unfortunately, the new wife did not at all resemble Awirehu. The latter had always been a good, kind, honest woman. The new wife was of a very jealous and selfish disposition. In addition to this, she was unable to walk normally, and continually imagined that people were making fun of her defect. She took the idea into her head that Ohia and Awirehu—when together—were in the habit of laughing at her. Nothing was further from their thoughts, but she refused to believe so. Whenever she saw them together, she would stand and listen outside the door to hear what they were saying. Of course, she never succeeded in hearing anything about herself.

At last, one evening, Ohia and Awirehu had gone to bed. The latter was fast asleep when Ohia heard a conversation which amused him very much. A couple of mice in one corner of the room were arranging to go to the larder to get some food, as soon as their master—who was watching them—was asleep. Ohia, thinking this was a good joke, laughed outright. His second wife heard him and rushed into the room. She thereupon accused him of making fun of her again to Awirehu. The astonished husband, of course, denied this, but to no purpose. The jealous woman insisted that, if he were laughing at an innocent joke, he would at once tell it to her. This Ohia could not do without breaking his promise to King Tiger. His refusal fully confirmed the second woman's suspicions, and she

did not rest till she had laid the whole matter before the chief. He, being an intimate friend of Ohia, tried to persuade him to reveal the joke and set the matter at rest. Ohia naturally was most unwilling to do anything of the sort. The persistent woman gave the chief no peace till he summoned her husband to answer her charge before the Assembly.

Finding no way of escape from the charge, Ohia prepared for death. He first called all his friends and relatives to a great feast and bade them farewell. Then he put his affairs in order—bequeathed all his gold to the faithful Awirehu, and his property to his son and servants. When he had finished, he went to the Assembly Place where the people of the neighborhood were gathered together.

He first took leave of the chief, and then commenced his tale. He related the story of his many misfortunes, of his adventure with the deer, and of his promise to King Tiger. Finally, he explained the cause of his laughter which had annoyed his wife. In so speaking he fell dead, as King Tiger had warned him.

He was buried amid great mourning, for everyone had liked and respected him. The jealous woman who had caused her husband's death was seized and burnt as a witch. Her ashes were then scattered to the four winds of heaven, and it is owing to this unfortunate fact that jealousy and selfishness are so widespread throughout the world, where before they scarcely existed.

Why Men and Women Don't Have Tails Like Cows

This tale was told by an African American storyteller named Uncle Ike to a white man who came to visit a lake near Tallahassee, Florida, in the early 1900s. It is one of many Adam and Eve stories that are told throughout Florida. This story is more humorous than the Genesis version since it incorporates a second theme about our relationship to an animal—in this case, the cow. The story is a myth based on an event that took place a long time ago as one way of explaining the origins of things. The story is basically religious prose that is handed down from generation to generation.

A long time ago, the good Lord made the world. And then he rested for a day. The next morning, he decided to plant a garden in the world. When he finished it, he called it the Garden of Eden. It was a beautiful, colorful garden with all kinds of flowers and trees. Fruits and berries grew on the trees and vines. He was pleased with what he had made.

Then one day he thought to himself that a garden needed somebody to live in it. So, he made Adam, the first man. Adam was kind of lonesome, so the good Lord took pity on him and made him a wife. Her name was Eve, and she was the first woman. Adam and Eve were just like men and women today, only they had great long tails like cows.

The tails were occasionally useful in that they could swat a troublesome fly or create a bit of a breeze when it was hot.

After Adam and Eve had seen the garden, God spoke to Adam. "Adam, this garden is for you and Eve. Stay here and take care of it. Use anything in it, and you may enjoy any of these fruits and berries." But then God pointed to another tree and said, "But you see this tree with the yellow fruit on it? Don't you touch that tree. It's mine."

Adam replied, "Yes Lord, I understand."

Not so long after having that conversation, God left the garden early one evening. Adam knew he was gone because he heard the garden gate go *click*. About that time, Adam was walking around, enjoying the flowers and shade trees, when he looked up and saw the forbidden tree with the yellow fruit! It was the one the Lord had told him not to touch.

Adam looked at it, and looked at it, and looked at it. The yellow fruit looked so lovely. He thought it must taste sweet and delicious. But Adam remembered God's words. This was God's fruit, and Adam was not to eat it. Although he tried to resist, Adam couldn't stop thinking about what that yellow fruit must taste like. At that moment, God's yellow fruit looked so much better than all the fruit on all the other trees. No other fruit seemed quite as special.

Adam became so tempted, he finally plucked one of the yellow fruits from God's tree. No longer able to resist, he stuffed it into his mouth. It tasted so delicious that he plucked another, then another and still another. Adam kept on eating and eating. After a few hours he had stuffed every piece of fruit on that tree in his mouth until there was no fruit left.

When Adam went to sleep that night, his belly was very full. He was so tired from eating all that fruit that he slept really hard. Adam kept on sleeping until late into the next day.

It was then that the Lord came back to the garden. Being God, he knew what Adam had done, and it made him really mad. God was so angry that Adam had eaten his fruit that he didn't even take the time to open the garden gate. He just put his hand on the wall and leaped over it. Then he went straight to the forbidden fruit tree.

When he got there and saw the tree, he was madder than ever. The previous night the tree had been full of ripe, beautiful fruit. This morning there was hardly a scrap of fruit to be seen. Every piece had been eaten. He looked again, and he saw that the dirt around the tree had been trampled down. He looked this way, and he looked that way. But he didn't see Adam or Eve. Adam had woken up just minutes before and decided he'd better not be around that tree when God returned to the garden.

The Lord called, "Adam." No answer. "Adam."

Adam hid behind a big oak tree and said nothing.

Then God called again, "Adam, you come here now!"

Adam figured he couldn't hide from God forever. God was too powerful. So, Adam came inching up to God, because he knew God knew what he had done. Adam was very afraid of what his punishment might be.

When Adam finally got to within a few feet of God, the Lord asked, "Adam, why did you eat the fruits from my tree?"

Adam looked at the ground, not wanting to own up to his bad deed. He scraped his foot in the dust and said, "It wasn't me. It was Eve."

God shook his head, further disappointed in Adam. He knew better than that. God told Adam, "That story won't work. Just look at the great big footprints around my tree. Eve's feet aren't that large."

Then Adam got scared, and he ran for the bushes. God quickly ran after him.

But Adam had trouble running. He couldn't go very fast because his long cow tail dragged way behind him in the dust. Adam had eaten so much he didn't have the strength to lift it from the ground. His tummy was still so full of the yellow fruit that he had to run with lots of extra weight. Still, he was very fearful of how God might punish him, so he ran and ran. Try as he did, he couldn't outrun God.

It didn't take too long for God to catch up with Adam, at least close enough to grab his tail. He grabbed it in his two hands, set his two heels into the ground, and pulled. The tail came right out of Adam's behind by the roots. Eve watched in amazement.

And that's why people today don't have tails like cows do.

How the Gopher Turtle Was Made

*This African American myth explains why there are two
kinds of turtles in Florida. One lives in the water; the
other is the gopher turtle, which lives on land. This story
is not only about the origin of things, but about naming
and the importance of communication. In many cultures,
creation is directly connected to speaking. In this story,
naming the turtle has a great deal to do with defining
what it is and where it lives. The gopher turtle is usually
referred to as a gopher tortoise. For some early white
settlers, the gopher tortoise was a delicacy they called
"scrub chicken." It is now illegal to kill and cook them.*

O ne day, God was sitting down by the ocean making
fish. He made a whale, threw it into the water, and it
swam off. He made a shark, threw it into the water, and it
swam off. He then made mullet and shad fish and trout, and
they all swam off.

While God was busy making his fish, the Devil was
standing behind him looking over his shoulder. The Devil
quietly watched for a while.

After making lots of fish, God made a turtle and threw
it into the water. It swam off. About then, the Devil said,
"I can make one of those things." The Devil thought a
turtle would be fairly easy to make.

God replied to the Devil, "No, I don't believe you can." God
knew that he was the creator of the world, and not the Devil.

The Devil insisted, "I can so make one of those things. Ain't nothing to making them anyhow. Who couldn't do that? I can't blow the breath of life into it, but I sure can make a turtle."

The Devil seemed so sure of himself that it made God a bit irritated. So, God decided to challenge the Devil. He said, "Devil. I know you can't make a turtle, but if you think you can, go ahead and make one, and I'll blow the breath of life into it for you."

You see, God was sitting down by the sea making fish out of sea-mud. But the Devil went on up to the hill so God wouldn't see him making his turtle. So, the Devil's turtle was made out of highland dirt.

God waited nearly all day before the Devil came back with his turtle made out of highland dirt.

As soon as God saw it, he said, "Devil, that isn't a turtle you've made."

The Devil flew into a rage. "This isn't a turtle? Who says it isn't a turtle? It sure is a turtle!"

God shook his head and said, "It sure isn't a turtle, but I'll blow the breath of life into it like I promised."

The Devil handed God the thing he called a turtle, and God blew the breath of life into what the Devil had made. Then God threw the highland dirt creature into the water. It came out. God threw him into the water again. He came out again. God threw him into the water a third time, and he came out a third time.

So, God said to the Devil, "I told you that wasn't a turtle." God knew that any real turtle would head for the sea.

Still, the Devil persisted. "Yes, sir, that is a turtle."

By this time God was chuckling a bit. He said, "Devil, don't you know that all turtles love the water? Don't you see what you made won't stay in the water?"

The Devil was stubborn, and he wasn't listening carefully to what God was saying. After all, the Devil mostly wanted to win the argument. He insisted again, "I keep telling you, I don't care if it doesn't go in the water. That's a turtle."

The debate continued for hours. Finally, the Devil became very tired. He realized that God was not going to give in and accept his highland dirt creature as a turtle. The Devil also knew he had to move on to other things. So, reluctantly, the Devil said, "Well, anyhow, it will go for one."

And that's why we have gopher turtles today!

How the Tortoise Got Its Shell

Another turtle tale, as tortoises are technically turtles, describes how it got to be formed as the reptile we now recognize. This Nigerian story begins as a hero's journey but has an unexpected ending. Although it could have a sad conclusion, it ends happily enough, providing us with an explanation on why tortoises have shells and why they are so slow. Regardless of their seeming limitations, turtles symbolize tranquility, longevity, and wisdom.

A few hundred years ago, the Chief Mauri (God) was determined to have a splendid yam festival. He therefore sent his messengers to invite all his chiefs and people to the gathering, which was to take place on Fida (Friday).

On the morning of that day, he sent some of his servants to the neighboring towns and villages to buy goats, sheep, and cows for the great feast. Mr. Klo (the tortoise), who was a tall and handsome fellow, was sent to buy palm wine. He was directed to the palm-fields of Koklovi (the chicken).

At that time, Klo was a very powerful traveler and speedily reached his destination, although it was many miles distant from Mauri's palace.

When he arrived, Koklovi was taking his breakfast. When they had exchanged polite salutations Koklovi asked the reason of Klo's visit. He replied, "I was sent by His Majesty, Chief Mauri, the ruler of the world, to buy him palm wine."

"Whether he's ruler of the world or not," answered Koklovi, "no one can buy my wine with money. If you want it, you must fight for it. If you win you can have it all and the palm trees too."

This answer delighted Klo as he was a very strong fighter. Koklovi was the same, so the fighting continued for several hours before Klo was able to overcome Koklovi. He was at last successful, however, and securely bound Koklovi before he left him.

Then, taking his great pot, he filled it with wine. Finding that there was more wine than the pot would hold, Klo foolishly drank all the rest. He then piled the palm trees on his back and set out for the palace with the pot of wine. The amount which he had drunk, however, made him feel so sleepy and tired that he could not walk fast with his load. Added to this, a terrible rain began to fall, which made the ground very slippery and difficult to travel over.

By the time Klo succeeded in reaching his master's palace the gates were shut and locked. Mauri, finding it so late, had concluded that everyone was inside.

There were many people packed into the great hall, and all were singing and dancing. The noise of the concert was so great that no one heard Klo's knocking at the gate, and there he had to stay with his great load of wine and palm trees.

The rain continued for nearly two months and was so terrible that the people all remained in the palace till it had finished. By that time Klo had died, under the weight of his load—which he had been unable to get off his back. There he lay, before the gate, with the pile of palm trees on top of him.

When the rain ceased and the gates were opened, the people were amazed to see this great mound in front of the gate, where before there had been nothing. They fetched spades and began to shovel it away.

When they came to the bottom of the pile there lay Klo. His earthenware pot and the dust had caked together and formed quite a hard cover on his back.

He was taken into the palace, and by the use of many wonderful medicines he was restored to life. But since that date he has never been able to stand upright. He has been a creeping creature, with a great shell on his back.

How Mushrooms First Grew

Folktales often move from one situation to another, demonstrating how one activity affects another, especially when something unexpected takes place. This tale, like many of the previous ones, is an origin story rooted in Africa. Anthills in Africa are large mounds, generally many feet high. Because of the richness of the dirt, mushrooms can grow in or around anthill mounds. While anthills in the United States are most often not as large, when mushrooms grow around anthills, it is because the climate is warm and moist.

Long, long ago, there dwelt in a town two brothers whose bad habits brought them much trouble. Day by day they fell more deeply in debt. Their creditors gave them no peace, so at last they ran away into the woods. They became highway robbers.

But they were not happy. Their minds were troubled by their evil deeds. At last, they decided to go home, make a big farm, and pay off their debts gradually.

They accordingly set to work and soon had quite a fine farm prepared for corn. As the soil was good, they hoped the harvest would bring in much money.

Unfortunately, that very day a bushfowl came along. Being hungry, it scratched up all the newly planted seeds and ate them.

The two poor brothers, on arriving at the field next day, were dismayed to find all their work quite wasted. They put down a trap for the thief. That evening the bushfowl was caught in it. The two brothers, when they came and found the bird, told it that now all their debts would be transferred to it because it had robbed them of the means of paying the debts themselves.

The poor bird—in great trouble at having such a burden thrust upon it—made a nest under a silk cotton tree. There it began to lay eggs, meaning to hatch them and sell the young birds for money to pay off the debt.

A terrible hurricane came, however, and a branch of the tree came down. All the eggs were smashed. As a result, the bushfowl transferred the debts to the tree, as it had broken the eggs.

The silk cotton tree was in dismay at having such a big sum of money to pay off. It immediately set to work to make as much silk cotton as it possibly could, that it might sell it.

An elephant, not knowing all that had happened, came along. Seeing the silk cotton, he came to the tree and plucked down all its bearings. By this means the debts were transferred to the poor elephant.

The elephant was very sad when he found what he had done. He wandered away into the desert, thinking of a way to make money. He could think of none.

As he stood quietly under a tree, a poor hunter crept up. This man thought he was very lucky to find such a fine elephant standing so still. He at once shot him.

Just before the animal died, he told the hunter that now the debts would have to be paid by him. The hunter was much grieved when he heard this, as he had no money at all.

He walked home wondering what he could do to make enough money to pay the debts. In the darkness he did not see the stump of a tree which the overseers had cut down in the road. He tripped over it and broke his leg. By this means the debts were transferred to the tree stump.

Not knowing this, a party of white ants came along the next morning and began to eat into the tree. When they had broken it nearly to the ground, the tree told them that now the debts were theirs, as they had killed it.

The ants, being very wise, held a council together to find out how best they could make money. They decided each to contribute as much as possible. With the proceeds one of their young men would go to the nearest market and buy pure linen thread. This they would weave and sell, and the profits would go to help pay the debts.

This was done. From time to time all the linen in stock was brought and spread out in the sunshine to keep it in good condition. When men see this linen lying out on the ant hills, they call it "mushroom," and gather it for food.

Why the Sun and the Moon
Live in the Sky

*In this Nigerian folktale, an explanation is given for
why we understand our solar system and our world
as we do. It is also a tale about friendship. Here, the
sun and moon are husband and wife. Perhaps this
tale is also about how having too much of what
you want can change the structure of friendship
and the world.*

Many years ago, the sun and water were great
friends, and both lived on the earth together. The
sun very often used to visit the water, but the water never
returned his visits. At last, the sun asked the water why it
was that he never came to see him in his house. The water
replied that the sun's house was not big enough, and that if
he came with his people he would drive the sun out.

He then said, "If you wish me to visit you, you must build
a very large compound; but I warn you that it will have to
be a tremendous place, as my people are very numerous,
and take up a lot of room."

The sun promised to build a very big compound, and
soon afterward he returned home to his wife, the moon, who
greeted him with a broad smile when he opened the door.
The sun told the moon what he had promised the water,
and the next day commenced building a huge compound in
which to entertain his friend.

When it was completed, he asked the water to come and visit him the next day.

When the water arrived, he called out to the sun, and asked him whether it would be safe for him to enter, and the sun answered, "Yes, come in, my friend."

The water then began to flow in, accompanied by the fish and all the water animals.

Very soon the water was knee-deep, so he asked the sun if it was still safe, and the sun again said, "Yes," so more water came in.

When the water was level with the top of a man's head, the water said to the sun, "Do you want more of my people to come?" and the sun and moon both answered, "Yes," not knowing any better. So the water flowed on, until the sun and moon had to perch themselves on the top of the roof.

Again, the water addressed the sun, but receiving the same answer, and more of his people rushing in, the water very soon overflowed the top of the roof, and the sun and moon were forced to go up into the sky, where they have remained ever since.

Why the Moon Waxes and Wanes

This origin story from Nigeria, explains why the moon looks different each day of the month. Today, the moon symbolizes many things, such as love, fertility, and a connection with nature through agriculture. The moon in this folktale includes several of these characteristics.

There was once an old woman who was very poor and lived in a small mud hut thatched with mats made from the leaves of the tombo palm in the bush. She was often very hungry, as there was no one to look after her.

In the olden days the moon used to come down to the earth often, although she lived most of the time in the sky. The moon was a fat woman with a skin of hide, and she was full of fat meat. She was quite round, and in the night used to give plenty of light. The moon was sorry for the poor starving old woman, so she came to her and said, "You may cut some of my meat away for your food." This the old woman did every evening, and the moon got smaller and smaller until you could scarcely see her at all. This made her give very little light, and all the people began to grumble in consequence, and to ask why the moon was getting so thin.

At last, the people went to the old woman's house where there happened to be a little girl sleeping. She had been there for only a little time and had seen the moon come down every evening. She watched the old woman go out with her knife and carve her daily supply of meat out of the moon. As she was very frightened, she told the people all about it, so they determined to set a watch on the movements of the old woman.

That night the moon came down as usual, and the old woman went out with her knife and basket to get her food; but before she could carve any meat, all the people rushed out shouting, and the moon was so frightened that she went back again into the sky, and never came down again to the earth. The old woman was left to starve in the bush.

Ever since that time, the moon has hidden herself most of the day, as she was so frightened, and she still gets very thin once a month, but later on she gets fat again, and when she is quite fat, she gives plenty of light all the night. This phase does not last very long, and she begins to get thinner and thinner, in the same way as she did when the old woman was carving her meat from her.

Why the Moon and Stars Receive Their Light from the Sun

We all know stories about castles, dragons, prisoners, and great escapes. This tale about Anansi's brilliant son, Kweku Tsin, has some similarities to the fairytales of "Rumpelstiltskin," "Rapunzel," and "Jack and the Beanstalk." Here, because Kweku Tsin is so courageous and inventive, he is given a great gift that involves shape-shifting, a common element in African folktales. Because of this getaway tale, we now know a lot more about how the universe we live in came to be.

Once upon a time, there was a great scarcity of food in the land. Father Anansi and his son, Kweku Tsin, being very hungry, set out one morning to hunt in the forest. In a short time Kweku Tsin was fortunate enough to kill a fine deer, which he carried to his father at their resting place. Anansi was very glad to see such a supply of food, and requested that his son remain there on guard, while he went for a large basket in which to carry it home. An hour or so passed without his return, and Kweku Tsin became anxious. Fearing that his father had lost his way, he called out loudly, "Father, father!" to guide him to the spot. To his joy he heard a voice reply, "Yes, my son," and immediately he shouted again, thinking it was Anansi. Instead of the latter, however, a terrible dragon appeared. This monster breathed fire from his great nostrils and was altogether a dreadful sight to behold. Kweku Tsin was terrified at his approach and speedily hid himself in a cave nearby.

The dragon arrived at the resting place and was much annoyed to find only the deer's body. He vented his anger in blows upon the animal's carcass and went away. Soon after, Father Anansi returned. He was deeply interested in his son's tale and wished to see the dragon for himself. He soon had his desire, for the monster, smelling human flesh, hastily returned to the spot and seized them both. They were carried off by him to his castle, where they found many other unfortunate creatures also awaiting their fate. All were left in the charge of the dragon's servant—a fine, white rooster—which always crowed to summon his master if anything unusual happened in the latter's absence. The dragon then went off in search of more prey.

Kweku Tsin summoned all his fellow prisoners together to orchestrate a way to escape. All were afraid to run away because of the wonderful powers of the monster. His eyesight was so keen that he could detect a fly moving miles away. Not only that, but he could move over the ground so swiftly that none could outdistance him. Kweku Tsin, however, being exceedingly clever, soon thought of a plan.

Knowing that the white rooster would not crow as long as he had grains of rice to pick up, Kweku scattered the contents of forty bags of grain that had been stored in the great hall on the ground. While the rooster was thus busily engaged, Kweku Tsin ordered the spinners to spin fine hempen ropes so they could make a strong rope ladder. He intended to throw up one end to heaven, trusting that the gods would catch it and hold it fast while he and his fellow prisoners climbed up.

While the ladder was being made, the men killed and ate all the cattle they needed—reserving all the bones for Kweku Tsin at his express desire. When all was ready, the young man gathered the bones into a great sack. He also procured the dragon's fiddle and placed it by his side.

Everything was now ready. Kweku Tsin threw one end of the ladder up to the sky. It was caught and held. The dragon's victims began to mount, one after the other, with Kweku remaining at the bottom.

By this time, however, the monster's powerful eyesight showed him that something unusual was happening at his abode. He hastened his return. On seeing his approach, Kweku Tsin also began to climb the ladder, with the bag of bones on his back and the fiddle under his arm. The dragon began to climb after him. Each time the monster came too near, the young man threw him a bone, and being very hungry, the dragon was obliged to descend to the ground to eat each one.

Kweku Tsin repeated this performance until all the bones were gone, by which time the people were safely up in the heavens. Then he ascended himself, as rapidly as possible, stopping every now and then to play a tune on the wonderful fiddle. Each time he did this, the dragon could not resist the magic music and had to return to earth to dance. When Kweku was quite close to the top, the dragon had very nearly reached him again. The brave youth bent down and cut the ladder away below his own feet. The dragon got caught in the rungs and dashed to

the ground—but Kweku was pulled up into safety by the gods.

The gods were so pleased with his wisdom and bravery in giving freedom to his fellow men, that they made him the sun—the source of all light and heat to the world. His father, Anansi, became the moon, and his friends the stars. Thereafter, it was Kweku Tsin's privilege to supply all these with light, each being dull and powerless without him.

MORALS TAUGHT THROUGH ANIMAL TALES

Animal tales are a traditional method of teaching morals to children. These tales each demonstrate different essential life lessons, such as the importance of making good decisions, always paying attention, and being selfless members of our communities. Many of these themes are highly relevant to the historical struggles of African Americans, teaching strategies to survive and navigate the world around them. In African folklore, we often see recurring animal characters such as the multifaceted Rabbit. In the Uncle Remus stories, animal behaviors and scenarios often reflect the struggles of life in slavery. Brer Rabbit, a notorious trickster, often upends the social order and serves as a resistance figure for those struggling to navigate unjust systems. Many of these animal tales present strategies to handle the issues of morality for enslaved African Americans, providing them with a source of support and solace. These tales offer entertainment for children and adults alike, sometimes in the form of rhyming poems.

The Squirrel and the Spider

Animal tales are often used to teach morals. Using the perspectives of two different animals to create a disagreement about ownership, this fable is about the consequences of stealing. However, the message is unclear, causing the reader to ponder its meaning as it demonstrates a quick turnaround of karma. Like most fables, this one is multidimensional.

A hardworking squirrel had, after much labor, succeeded in cultivating a very fine farm. Being a skillful climber of trees, he had not troubled to make a roadway into his farm. He reached it by the trees.

One day, when his harvests were very nearly ripe, it happened that Spider went out hunting in that neighborhood. During his travels, he arrived at Squirrel's farm. Greatly pleased at the appearance of the fields, he sought the roadway to it. Finding none, he returned home and told his family all about the matter. The very next day they all set out for this fine place and set to work immediately to make a road. When this was completed, Spider—who was very cunning—threw pieces of earthenware pot along the pathway. This he did to make believe that his children had dropped them while working to prepare the farm.

Then he and his family began to cut down and carry away as much of the corn as was ripe. Squirrel noticed that his fields were being robbed but could not at first find the thief. He decided to watch. Sure enough, Spider soon reappeared to steal more of the harvest. Squirrel demanded to know what right he had on these fields. Spider immediately asked him the same question. "They are my fields," said Squirrel.

"Oh, no! They are mine," retorted Spider.

"I dug them and sowed them and planted them," said poor Squirrel.

"Then where is your roadway to them?" said crafty Spider.

"I need no roadway. I come by the trees," was Squirrel's reply.

Spider laughed scornfully in response and continued to use the farm as his own.

Squirrel appealed to the law, but the court determined that no one had ever had a farm without a road leading to it, therefore the fields must be Spider's.

With great glee Spider and his family prepared to cut down all the harvest that remained. When it was cut, they tied it in great bundles and set off to the nearest marketplace to sell it. When they were about halfway there, a terrible storm came on. They were forced to put down their burdens by the roadside and run for shelter. When the storm had passed they returned to pick up their loads.

As they approached the spot, they found a great, black crow there, with his broad wings outspread to keep the bundles dry. Spider went to him and very politely thanked him for so kindly taking care of their property. "Your property!" replied Father Crow. "Who ever heard of anyone leaving bundles of corn by the roadside? Nonsense! These loads are mine." So, saying, he picked them up and went off with them, leaving Spider and his children to return home sorrowful and empty-handed. Their thieving ways had brought them little profit.

The Leopard and the Ram

Sometimes, folktales are based on secrets and misunderstandings. In this tale, good friends who have different ways of hunting lose their friendship due to a lack of sharing their differences. It offers the reader a moral about trust and the damage secrets can do.

A ram once decided to make a clearing in the woods and build himself a house. A leopard who lived near also made up his mind to do the very same thing.

Unbeknownst to each other, they both chose the same site. Ram came one day and worked at the clearing. Leopard arrived after Ram had gone and was much surprised to find some of his work already done. However, he continued what Ram had begun. Each was surprised daily by the progress made in his absence, but each concluded that the fairies had been helping him. They gave their helpers thanks and continued with their tasks.

Thus, the matter went on—the two working alternately at the building and never seeing one another. At last, the house was finished to the satisfaction of both.

The two prepared to take up their abode as their new home.

To their great astonishment, they met. Each told his tale, and after some friendly discussion, they decided to live together.

Both Leopard and Ram had sons. These two young animals played together while their parents hunted. Leopard was very surprised to find that every evening his friend Ram brought home just as much meat or venison from the hunt as he himself did. He did not dare to ask the other how he obtained it.

One day, before setting out to hunt, Leopard requested his son find out from young Ram how his father managed to kill the animals. Accordingly, while they were playing, little Leopard inquired how Father Ram, having neither claws nor sharp teeth, succeeded in catching and killing the beasts. Young Ram refused to tell unless young Leopard would promise to show his father's way as well. The latter agreed. Accordingly, they took two large pieces of plantain stem and set out into the woods.

Young Leopard then took one piece and placed it in position. Then, going first to the right, then to the left—posturing and peeping at the stem just as his father did—he took aim, sprang toward the stem, and tore it.

Young Ram then took the other piece of stem and placed it in position. Wasting no time, he went backed up, took aim, then ran swiftly forward—pushing his head against the stem and splitting it to pieces. When they were both satisfied, they swept the place clean and went home.

In the evening Leopard obtained all the information about the hunt from his son. The latter warned him that he must always be careful when he saw Ram go backward. He kept this in mind, and from that day watched Ram very closely.

Sometime afterward, it rained and made the floor of the house very slippery. The leopard called the ram, as usual, to dine with him. As he was coming, the ram slipped backward on the wet floor. The leopard, seeing this, thought the other was about to kill him. Calling to his son to follow, he sprang with all his might over the wall of the house and fled to the woods. The ram called him back, but he did not listen. From that time leopards have made their abode in the woods while rams have remained at home.

To Lose an Elephant for the Sake of a Wren is a Very Foolish Thing to Do

Folktales often teach morals about the folly of making poor decisions. This tale begins with the King's pledge of gifting an elephant to whomever can chop down a huge tree with a wooden axe. Traditionally, elephants represent wisdom and strength, both physical and mental. For some, they are viewed as human chiefs from the past. It is no surprise that these majestic animals are valued by humans. After Spider tricks the King, he receives the promised elephant. But silly Spider is diverted by a wren who will provide him with far less food than the elephant. One thing we learn from this story is that we should be careful about easily being distracted and wrongly thinking we can have it all.

In the olden times, a great tree stood in the King's town. This tree was so huge that it began to overshadow the neighboring fields. The King decided to have it cut down. He requested that his servants proclaim throughout the country that anyone who succeeded in cutting down the tree with a wooden axe should receive an elephant as payment.

People thought it would be impossible to cut down such a great tree with an axe of wood. Spider decided to try using his cunning to gain the elephant. He presented himself before the King and expressed his readiness to get rid of the tree.

A servant was sent with him to keep watch and to see that he only used the wooden axe given to him. Spider, however, had taken care to have another, made of steel, hidden in his bag.

He then began to chop down the tree. In very little time, he said to the servant, "See, yonder is a fine antelope. If you are quick, you will be able to hit it with a stone. Run!" The lad did as he was bid and ran a long way—but could see no sign of the antelope. In his absence, Spider seized the sharp axe and hastened to cut as much of the tree as he could, carefully hiding the axe in his bag before the servant's return.

He repeated the trick several times, till finally the tree was cut down. Spider went to the King to receive his elephant and brought along the servant to vouch that he had used only the wooden axe. He got his promised reward and started for home in great glee. On the way, however, he began to think over the matter. "Shall I take this animal home?" thought he. "That would be foolish, for then I would be obliged to share it with my family. No! I will hide it in the forest and eat it at my leisure. In that way I can have the whole of it for myself. Now what can I take home for the children's dinner?"

Thereupon he looked around, and, a little distance away, saw a tiny wren sitting on a tree. "Exactly what I want," he said to himself. "That will be quite sufficient for them. I will tie my elephant to this tree while I catch the bird."

This he did, but when he tried to seize the wren, it flew off. He chased it for some time, without success. "Well, well!" said he. "My family will just have to go without dinner. I will now go back and get my elephant." He returned to the spot where he had left the animal, but to his dismay, it had escaped. Spider was obliged to go home empty-handed, and he, as well as his family, went dinnerless that day.

Why the Leopard Can Only Catch Prey on Its Left Side

While the leopard is usually depicted as the most noble, elegant, and graceful of all the African cats, the one in this story is foolish and unwise. He goes to Cat to learn to hunt, but because he fails to value the kindness of his teacher, he is relegated to being a very debilitated hunter. One can only imagine how strange he must look when trying to catch his prey.

At one time, leopards did not know how to catch animals for food. Knowing that Cat was very skillful in this way, Leopard one day went to Cat and asked very politely if she would teach him the art. Cat readily consented.

The first thing Leopard had to learn was to hide himself among the bushes by the roadside, so that he would not be seen by any animal passing by. Next, he needed to learn how to move noiselessly through the woods. He must never allow the animal he chased to know that he was following it. The third great principle was how to use his left paws and side in springing upon his prey.

Having taught him these three things, Cat requested that Leopard go and practice them well. Once he had learned them thoroughly, he could return to her, and she would give him more lessons in hunting.

Leopard obeyed. At first he was very successful and obtained all the food he wanted. One day, however, he was unable to catch anything at all.

Being very hungry, he pondered what he could have for dinner. Suddenly, he remembered that Cat had quite a large family. He went straight to her home and found her absent.

Never thinking of her kindness to him—Leopard only remembered that he was hungry—he ate all her kittens. Cat, on discovering this dreadful fact, was so angry that she refused to have anything more to do with the great creature.

Consequently, the leopard has never been able to learn how to catch animals that pass him on the right side.

The Lion and the Wolf

Instead of the wolf in sheep's clothing depicted in "Little Red Riding Hood," this folktale has a lion pretending to be a sheep to trick a wolf. The lion, known for being a fierce predator with great speed and stealth, can also demonstrate exceptional judgment in practical matters. In this tale, he shows a kindness for a widow while displaying his prowess as a hunter. In African American folklore, the wolf often represents the white power structure of the masters or overseers.

A certain old lady had a very fine flock of sheep. She had fed and cared for them so well that they became famous for their fatness. In time, a wicked wolf heard of them and determined to eat them.

Night after night he stole up to the old dame's cottage and killed a sheep. The poor woman tried her best to save her animals from harm—but failed.

At last, there was only one sheep left of all the flock. Their owner was very sad. She feared that it, too, would be taken away from her, in spite of all she could do. While she was grieving over the thought of this, a lion came to her village.

Seeing her sad face, he asked the reason for it. She soon told him all about it. He thereupon offered to do his best to punish the wicked wolf. He himself went to the place where the sheep were generally kept—while the latter were removed to another place.

In the meantime, the wolf was on his way to the cottage. As he came, he met a fox. The fox was somewhat afraid of him and prepared to run away. The wolf, however, told him where he was going, and invited him to go too. The fox agreed and the two set off together. They arrived at the cottage and went straight to the place where the sheep generally slept. The wolf at once rushed upon the animal, while Fox waited a little behind. Just as Fox was deciding to enter and help Wolf, there came a bright flash of lightning. By the light of it the fox could see that the wolf was attacking—not a sheep—but a lion. He hastily ran away, shouting as he went, "Look at his face! Look at his face!"

During the flash, Wolf did look at the pretended sheep. To his dismay he found he had made a great mistake. At once he began to make humble apologies—but all in vain. Lion refused to listen to any of his explanations, and speedily put him to death.

Rabbit Rides Wolf

Rabbit, used to being the center of attention, is not happy when some girls pay more attention to Wolf. In order to change the narrative, Rabbit tells a lie to the girls and more lies to Wolf. He continues to trick Wolf as he ingratiates himself with the girls. When Wolf finally understands Rabbit's bad character, he goes after him to teach him a lesson. In the end, however, Rabbit lies again, and Wolf pays the price.

Some girls lived not far from Rabbit and Wolf, and Rabbit thought he would like to visit them. So, one time he called upon Wolf and said, "Let us go visiting."

Wolf said, "All right," and they started off.

When they got to the place, the girls told them to sit down and they took a great liking to Wolf, who had a good time with them while Rabbit had to sit by and look on.

Of course, he was not pleased at this turn of affairs and said, "We had better be going back."

But Wolf replied, "Let us wait a while longer," and they remained until it was late.

Before they left, Rabbit got a chance to speak to one of the girls where Wolf could not overhear, and he said, "The one you are having so much sport with is my old horse."

"I think you are lying," said the girl.

"I am not. You shall see me ride him up here tomorrow."

"If we see you ride him up to us, we'll believe you."

When they started off, the girls said, "Well, call again." Wolf was anxious to do so and early next morning be called upon Rabbit, whose house was much nearer, and said, "Are we going?"

"I was sick all night," Rabbit answered, "and I hardly feel able to go." Wolf urged him, but he said at first that he really wasn't able to.

Finally, however, he said, "If you will let me ride you, I might go along just for company." So, Wolf agreed to carry him astride of his back. But then Rabbit said, "I would like to put a saddle on you so as to brace myself," and Wolf agreed to it. "I believe it would be better," added Rabbit, "if I should bridle you." Wolf did not like this idea, but Rabbit said, "Then I could hold on better and won't fall off." So, Wolf finally consented to be bridled. Finally, Rabbit wanted to put on spurs.

Wolf replied, "I am too ticklish."

Rabbit said, "I will not spur you on with them. I will hold them away from you, but it would be nicer to have them on."

And so, Wolf finally agreed, saying only, "I am very ticklish; you must not spur me."

"When we get near the house," said Rabbit, "we will take everything off of you and walk the rest of the way."

Thus, Rabbit and Wolf started on, but when they were nearly in sight of the house Rabbit plunged the spurs into Wolf and before he knew it, they had passed right by the house. Then Rabbit said, "They have seen you now. I will tie you here and go up to see them and come back after a while and let you go."

Rabbit went to the house and said to the girls, "You all saw it, did you not?"

"Yes," they answered, and he sat down and had a good time with them.

After a while, Rabbit thought he ought to let Wolf go and started back to the place where he was fastened. He knew that Wolf was angry with him and thought up a way by which he could let him loose him safely. First, he found a thin hollow log which he beat upon as if it were a drum. Then he ran up to Wolf as fast as he could go and cried out, "Do you know they are hunting for you? You heard the drum just now. The soldiers are after you."

Wolf was very frightened and said, "Let me go."
Rabbit was purposely a little slow in untying him and he
had barely gotten him freed when Wolf broke away and
went off as fast as he could run. Then Rabbit returned
to the house and remained there as if he were already
a married man.

Near this house was a large peach orchard, and one
day Rabbit said to the girls, "I will shake the peaches off
for you." They all went to the orchard together and he
climbed up into a tree to shake the peaches off.

While he was there, Wolf came toward them and called
out, "Old fellow, I am not going to let you alone." By that
time, he was almost under the tree. Then Rabbit shouted out
loud as if to people at a distance, "Here is that fellow for
whom you are always hunting," and Wolf ran away again.

Some time after this, while Rabbit was lying close under
a tree bent over near the ground, he saw Wolf coming.
Then he stood up with the tree extended over his shoulder
as if he were trying to hold it up. When Wolf saw him, he
said, "I have you now." Rabbit, however, called out, "They
told me to hold this tree up all day with the great power
I have, and for it, they would give me four hogs. I don't
like hog meat, but you do, so you might get it if you take
my place." Wolf's greed was excited by this and he was
willing to hold up the tree. Then Rabbit said, "If you yield
only a little it will give way, so you must hold it tight." And
then he ran off.

Wolf stood under the tree so long that finally he felt
he could stand it no longer and he jumped away quickly
so that it would not fall upon him. Then he saw that it

was a growing tree rooted in the earth. "That Rabbit is the biggest liar," he exclaimed. "If I can catch him, I will certainly fix him."

After that, Wolf hunted about for Rabbit once more and finally came upon him in a nice grassy place. He was about to spring upon him when Rabbit said, "My friend, don't punish me. I have food for you. There is a horse lying out yonder." Wolf's appetite was again moved at the prospect and he decided to go along. Then Rabbit said, "It is pretty close to a house; therefore, it would be well for me to tie your tail to the horse's tail so that you can drag it off to a place where you can feast at leisure." So, Rabbit tied the two tails together. But the horse was only asleep—not dead, as Wolf supposed—and Rabbit ran around to its head and kicked it. At once the horse jumped up and was so frightened that it kicked and kicked until it kicked Wolf to death.

King Chameleon and the Animals

Some folktales, like this one, resonate strongly with people today because they pose questions about how we live, when rules are necessary, and who rulers should be. We learn that winning might be a losing proposition. As chameleons are known for changing their colors, metaphorically, sometimes people do as well.

In the olden days all the animals of the world lived together in friendship. They had no one to rule over them and judge them. Consequently, many very wicked deeds were constantly being done because no one feared any punishment.

At last, all the animals met together to discuss this bad state of affairs, and, as a result, they decided to choose a king. The great difficulty was how to choose him.

Lion was the first animal suggested. But all opposed him because they said he was too fierce. Wolf was next named—but the sheep and goats refused to have him because he was their foe. They knew he would treat them badly if he was chosen.

As it was impossible to please everyone, they decided in another way. Two miles away was a great stool placed under a very ancient tree which they believed to be the abode of some of their gods. They would have a great race. The animal which reached the stool first and sat down would be chosen king.

The day of the race arrived. All animals, great and small, prepared to take part in it. The signal being given, they started off. The hare—being a very fine runner—speedily outdistanced the others. He reached the stool quite five hundred yards ahead of the next animal. You may judge of his annoyance when, just as he was going to sit down, a voice came from the stool saying, "Take care, Mr. Hare, take care. I was here first." This was the chameleon. He, being able to change his color to suit his surroundings, had seized Mr. Hare's tail just as the race began. Having made his color match the hare's, no one had noticed him. He had held on very tightly, and when Mr. Hare turned round to take his seat Chameleon dropped off and landed on the stool.

The hare saw how he had been tricked and was very angry. The other animals, however, arrived before he could harm the chameleon. According to the agreement they had made, they had no choice but to make Mr. Chameleon king.

But none of the animals were satisfied with the choice. So, as soon as the meeting was over, all scattered in every direction and left Mr. Chameleon quite alone.

He was so ashamed that he went and made his home at the top of a very high tree on a mountain. In the dead of night you may hear him calling his attendants to come and stay with him. But he is left quite alone. "A king without subjects is no king."

The Creeturs Go to the Barbecue

Told in dialect, this Brother Rabbit (commonly called Brer Rabbit) story demonstrates the storytelling process with Uncle Remus as the teller and a listener who soon becomes part of the tale. The storyteller sets the stage in a long-ago time, a frequent way to start folktales of many kinds where the timing is in the past but it's unclear how long ago it was. As usual, Brer Rabbit is stirring up trouble. This tale includes many other Uncle Remus characters besides Brer Rabbit such as Mr. Man, Brer Wolf, Brer Coon, Brer B'ar (Bear), a pack of dogs, and snake doctors.

"**O**nce 'pon a time," said Uncle Remus to the little boy.

"But when was once upon a time?" the child interrupted to ask.

The old man smiled. "I speck 'twuz one time er two times, er maybe a time an' a half. You know when Johnny Ashcake 'gun ter bake? Well, 'twuz 'long in dem days. Once 'pon a time," he resumed, "Mr. Man had a gyarden so fine dat all de neighbors come ter see it. Some 'ud look at it over de fence, some 'ud peep thoo de cracks, an' some 'ud come an' look at it by de light er de stars. An' one un um wuz ol' Brer Rabbit; starlight, moonlight, cloudlight, de nightlight wuz de light fer him. When de turn er de mornin' come, he 'uz allers up an' about, an' a-feelin' purty well I thank you, suh!

"Now, den, you done hear what I say. Dar wuz Mr.

Man, yander wuz de gyarden, an' here wuz ol' Brer Rabbit." Uncle Remus made a map of this part of the story by marking in the sand with his walking cane. "Well, dis bein' de case, what you speck gwineter happen? Nothin' in de roun' worl' but what been happenin' sence greens an' sparrer-grass wuz planted in de groun'. Dey look fine an' dey tas'e fine, an' long to'rds de shank er de mornin', Brer Rabbit 'ud creep thoo de crack er de fence an' nibble at um. He'd take de greens, but leave his tracks, mo' speshually right atter a rain. Takin' an' leavin'—it's de way er de worl'.

"Well, one mornin', Mr. Man went out in his truck patch, an' he fin' sump'n missin'—a cabbage here, a turnip dar, an' a mess er beans yander, an' he ax how come dis? He look 'roun', he did, an' he seed Brer Rabbit's tracks what he couldn't take wid 'im. Brer Rabbit had lef' his shoes at home, an' come bar'footed.

"So, Mr. Man, he call his dogs 'Here, Buck! Here, Brinjer! Here, Blue!' An' he sicc'd um on de track, an' here dey went!

"You'd 'a' thunk dey wuz runnin' atter forty-lev'm rhinossyhosses fum de fuss dey made. Brer Rabbit he hear um comin' an' he put out fer home, kinder doublin' 'roun' des like he do deze days.

"When he got ter de p'int whar he kin set down fer ter rest his face an' han's, he tuck a poplar leaf an' 'gun ter fan hisse'f. Den Brer Fox come a-trottin' up. He say, 'Brer Rabbit, what's all dis fuss I hear in de woods? What de name er goodness do it mean?' Brer Rabbit kinder scratch his head an' 'low, 'Why, deyer tryin' fer drive me ter de big bobbycue on de creek. Dey all ax me, an' when I 'fuse dey say deyer gwine ter make me go any how. Dey ain't no fun in bein' ez populous ez what I is, Brer Fox. Ef you wanter go, des git in ahead er de houn's an' go lickity-split down de big road!'

"Brer Fox roll his little eyes, an' lick his chops whar he dribble at de mouf, an put out ter de bobbycue, an' he ain't mo' dan made his disappearance, 'fo' here come Brer Wolf, an' when he got de news, off he put.

"An' he ain't mo'n got out'n sight, 'fo' here come ol' Brer B'ar, an' when he hear talk er de bakin' meat an' de big pan er gravy, he sot up on his behime legs an' snored. Den off he put, an' he ain't got out'n hearin', 'fo' Brer Coon come rackin' up, an' when he got de news, he put out.

"So dar dey wuz an' what you gwine do 'bout it? It seem like dey all got in front er de dogs, er de dogs got behime um, an' Brer Rabbit sot by de creek-side laughin' an' hittin' at de snake doctors. An' dem po' creeturs had ter go clean past de bobbycue—ef dey wuz any bobbycue, which I don't skacely speck dey wuz. Dat what make me say what I does—when you git a invite ter a bobbycue, you better fin' out when an' whar it's at, an' who runnin' it."

Brer Rabbit's Frolic

After the barbecue, the creatures limped home as best they could, hoping that at a later time they could get the better of Brer Rabbit. But their game plan never seems to work out, as Brer Rabbit knows all about their schemes. This tale introduces Cousin Rain and Brer Dust, creating a further association with the natural world. In these Uncle Remus tales, which are allegories, Brer Rabbit represents the Black enslaved person's alter ego, whereas the stronger animals represent the white enslaver. The trickster's goal here, and in other Brer Rabbit stories, is to upend the social order as issues of morality are presented.

After hearing how the animals went to the barbecue, the little boy wanted to know what happened to them when next he saw Uncle Remus. He was anxious to learn if any of them were hurt by the dogs that had been chasing Brer Rabbit. The old man closed his eyes and chuckled. "You sho is axin' sump'n now, honey. Und' his hat, ef he had any, Brer Rabbit had a mighty quick-thinkin' apple-ratus, an' mos' inginner'lly, all de time, de pranks he played on de yuther creeturs pestered um bofe ways a-comin' an' a-gwine. De dogs done mighty well, 'long ez dey had dealin's wid de small fry, like Brer Fox, an' Brer Coon, an' Brer Wolf, but when dey run ag'in' ol' Brer B'ar, dey sho struck a snag. De mos' servigrous wuz de identual one dat got de wust hurted.

He got too close ter Brer B'ar, an' when he look at hisse'f in runnin' water, he tuck notice dat he wuz split wide open fum flank ter dewlap.

"Atter de rucus wuz over, de creeturs hobbled off home de best dey could, an' laid 'roun' in sun an' shade fer ter let der cuts an' gashes git good an' well. When dey got so dey could segashuate, an' pay der party calls, dey 'gree fer ter insemble some'rs, an' hit on some plan fer ter outdo Brer Rabbit. Well, dey had der insembly, an' dey jower'd an' jower'd des like yo' pa do when he ain't feelin' right well; but, bimeby, dey 'greed 'pon a plan dat look like it mought work. Dey 'gree fer ter make out dat dey gwine ter have a dance. Dey know'd dat ol' Brer Rabbit wuz allers keen fer dat, an' dey say dey'll gi' him a invite, an' when he got dar, dey'd ax 'im fer ter play de fiddle, an' ef he 'fuse, dey'll close in on 'im an' make way wid 'im.

"So fur, so good! But all de time dey wuz jowerin' an' confabbin', ol' Brer Rabbit wus settin' in a shady place in de grass, a-hearin' eve'y word dey say. When de time come, he crope out, he did, an' run 'roun', an' de fust news dey know'd, here he come down de big road—bookity-bookity—same ez a hoss dat's broke thoo de pastur' fence. He say, sezee, 'Why, hello, frien's! An' howdy, too, kaze I ain't seed you-all sence de last time! Whar de name er goodness is you been deze odd-come-shorts? An' how did you far' at de bobbycue? Ef my two eyeballs ain't gone an' got crooked, dar's ol' Brer B'ar, him er de short tail an' sharp tush—de ve'y one I'm a-huntin' fer! An' dar's Brer Coon! I sho is in big luck. Dar's gwineter be a big frolic at Miss Meadows', an' her an' de gals want Brer B'ar fer ter show um de roas'n'-y'ar shuffle; an' dey put Brer Coon down fer de jig dey calls rack-back-Davy.

"'I'm ter play de fiddle—sump'n I ain't done sence my oldest gal had de mumps an' de measles, bofe de same day an' hour! Well, dis mornin', I tuck down de fiddle fum whar she wuz a-hangin' at, an' draw'd de bow backerds an' forerds a time er two, an' den I shot my eyes an' hit some er de ol'-time chunes, an' when I come ter myse'f, dar wuz my whole blessed fambly skippin' an' sasshayin' 'roun' de room, spite er de fack dat brekkus wuz ter be cooked!'

"Wid dat, Brer Rabbit bow'd, he did, an' went back down de road like de dogs wuz atter 'im."

"But what happened then?" the little boy asked.

"Nothin' 't all," replied Uncle Remus, taking up the chuckle where he had left off. "De creeturs ain't had no dance, an' when dey went ter Miss Meadows', she put her head out de winder, an' say ef dey don't go off fum dar she'll have de law on um!"

Brer Rabbit Finds the Moon
in the Mill Pond

*This Brer Rabbit tale is told in rhyme. It is a hilarious
story about what happens when you see something
that isn't real. Told as a poem, it is an allegory with a
hidden meaning. In his usual form, Brer Rabbit takes
advantage of other animals, this time with a dare.
If the moon is lost by falling in the water, there will be
no light during the night. Therefore, someone has to
take responsibility to save the moon. As is often the
case, Uncle Remus's colorful characters are placed
in unfamiliar territory.*

Oh, one bright day in de middle er May,
Brer Rabbit wuz feelin' fine;
He tuck ter de road, an' never know'd
De place whar he wuz gwine!

"Oh, fur an' free," sezee, "siree,
No gal kin change my min'!"
Brer Tarrypin, sly, he wunk one eye,
Un'neat' his green-gourd vine!

He holla an' say, "Whar you gwine dis day,
Wid yo' pipe an' walkin'-cane?"
Brer Rabbit wave his han' like a gal do her fan—
"My heart's 'bout ter bust wid pain;

"I'm a heap too nice, I ain't laugh'd but twice
Sence de big Jinawary rain;
My day'll be done ef I don't have some fun—
Dey'll call me Sunday-Jane!

"I'll git sollumcholic ef I don't have a frolic,
My head'll git flabby an' swink;
I chaw de pine-bud, kaze I'm 'bout ter lose my cud
An' some nights I don't sleep a wink!

"Ef I has ter set still, oh, I'll w'ar de green willow,
An' go in mo'nin' wid de Mink!
But I bet you a hat dat 'fo' I does dat,
I'll show um all a new kink!"

So, off he put, on his nimbles' foot,
Wid a grin, a laugh, an' a cough;
Ter Miss Motts an' Miss Meadows, an' all de udders,
He tell what 'uz gwineter come off!

'Twuz a mill-pon' fishin', an' he lef um a-wishin'
Dat de win' don't blow fum de norf!
An' de creeturs all, bofe long an' tall—
An' dem no bigger dan a dwarf—

Brer Wolf an' Brer B'ar all say dey'd be dar,
An' dey promise fer ter fetch a seine;
Dey 'gree ter de day, an' Brer Rabbit say
Dat dey don't hatter come ef it rain;

So said, so done, an' when de time come,
De big road ez well ez de lane
Wuz filled wid a crowd, all talkin' out loud,
An' a-prankin' wid might an' main!

Brer Rabbit wuz dar, wid Miss Molly Har',
A-waitin' fer de fun ter begin;
He shuck his shank, an' went ter de bank,
An' make like he gwineter jump in!

But de sight dat he saw made 'im drap his jaw,
An' break up a great big grin!
He sez ter Brer Coon, "Run here an' see de Moon!
A-floatin' widout a fin!"

He look ag'in—"She sho fell in,
An' we got ter git her out;
Ef she stays in de pon', it's 'Good-bye, John!'
An' uv dat dey ain't no doubt;

"We got ter have light when we play at night,
Fer ter see how ter git about;
We'll drag wid de seine—ef we don't drag in vain,
We'll have good reason ter shout!"

But when it come ter seinin', dar wuz some complainin
'Bout who wuz ter do it all,
Dey all make out dat dey wanter wade out,
But it fell on dem dat wuz tall:
Brer B'ar, he laugh, ez he tuck a staff,

Brer Wolf say he fear'd he'd fall,
But he tuck his place wid a mighty wry face,
An' when dey 'gun ter haul.

"Oh, you better bet dis water's wet!
I feel des like a sponge!"
An' den dey all, wid a kick an' a squall,
Wid a squeal an' den a lunge,

Grabbed at de water—which dey hadn't oughter
Went over der heads wid a splunge;
Brer Rabbit bent double, "Oh, all er yo' trouble
Fills me full er fun-unj-unj!"

Brother Bear's Big House

This Uncle Remus folktale focuses on Brer B'ar (also known as Brother Bear) who owns a comfortable home with his family. They happily have food, warmth, and each other. But what happens when someone who is not a bear asks for entry? Is Brer Polecat let in, or does he find his own way inside? Although the ending is humorous, the tale has political and sociological overtones. Folktales such as this one were important to African Americans during the times of slavery because they offered strategies for navigating an unjust system.

"**U**v all de creeturs," said Uncle Remus, in response to a questioning took on the part of the little boy, "ol Brer B'ar had de biggest an' de warmest house. I dunner why ner wharfo', but I'm a-tellin' you de plain fack, des ez dey to! It unter me. Ef I kin he'p it, I never will be deceivin' you, ner lead you inter no bad habits. Yo' pappy trotted wid me a mighty long time, an' ef you'll ax him he'll tell you dat de one thing I never did do wuz ter deceive him whiles he had his eyes open; not ef I knows myse'f. Well, ol' Brer B'ar had de big house I'm a-tellin' you about. Ef he y'ever is brag un it, it ain't never come down ter me. Yit dat's des what he had—a big house an' plenty er room fer him an' his fambly; an' he ain't had mo' dan he need, kaze all er his fambly wuz fat an' had what folks calls heft—de nachal plunkness.

"He had a son name Simmon, an' a gal name Sue, not countin' his ol' 'oman, an' dey all live wid one an'er day atter day, an' night atter night; an' when one un um went abroad, dey'd be spected home 'bout meal-time, ef not befo', an' dey segashuated right along fum day ter day, washin' der face an' han's in de same wash-pan in de back po'ch, an' wipin' on de same towel same ez all happy famblies allers does.

"Well, time went on an' fotched de changes dat might be spected, an' one day dar come a mighty knockin' on Brer B'ar's do'. Brer B'ar, he holla out, he did. 'Who dat come a-knockin' dis time er de year, 'fo' de corn's done planted, er de cotton-crap's pitched?' De one at de do' make a big noise, an' rattle de hinges. Brer B'ar holla out, he did, 'Don't t'ar down my house! Who is you, anyhow, an' what you want?' An' de answer come, 'I'm one an'

darfo' not two; ef youer mo' dan one, who is you an' what you doin' in dar?' Brer B'ar, he say, sezee, 'I'm all er one an' mighty nigh two, but I'd thank you fer ter tell me yo' full fambly name.' Den de answer come.

"'I'm de knocker an' de mover bofe, an' ef I can't clim' over I'll crawl under ef you do but gi' me de word. Some calls me Brer Polecat, an' some a big word dat it ain't wuff while ter ermember, but I wanter move in. It's mighty col' out here, an' all I meets tells me it's mighty warm in dar whar you is.' Den ol' Brer B'ar say, sezee. 'It's warm nuff fer dem what stays in here, but not nigh so warm fer dem on de outside. What does you reely want?' Brer Polecat 'spon', he did, 'I wants a heap er things dat I don't git. I'm a mighty good housekeeper, but I takes notice dat dar's mighty few folks dat wants me ter keep house fer um.' Brer B'ar say, sezee, 'I ain't got no room fer no housekeeper; we ain't skacely got room fer ter go ter bed. Ef you kin keep my house on de outside, you er mighty welcome.'

"Brer Polecat say, 'You may think you ain't got no room, but I bet you got des ez much room ez anybody what I know. Ef you let me in dar one time, I boun' you I'll make all de room I want.'"

Uncle Remus paused to see what effect this statement would have on the little boy. He closed his eyes, as though he were tired, but when he opened them again, he saw the faint shadow of a smile on the child's face. "'Taint gwine ter hurt you fer ter laugh a little bit, honey. Brer Polecat come in Brer B'ar's house, an' he had sech a bad breff dat dey all hatter git out—an' he stayed an' stayed twel time stopped runnin' ag'in' him."

How Mr. Lion Lost his Wool

This Uncle Remus tale begins with Mr. Man deciding to have a hog killing. After boiling the hogs in a large barrel, the next step is to remove the hog's hair by scraping the carcass. When Brer Rabbit says he's going to take a bath in the barrel used to boil the hogs, Mr. Lion shows up and decides he too wants a bath. What happens next explains why lions are the way they are and why it isn't a good idea to listen to Brer Rabbit.

"**T**wuz des sech a day ez dis dat Mr Lion lost his wool," remarked Uncle Remus to the little boy, "Mr. Man tuck a notion dat de time done come fer him fer ter have a hog-killin' an' he got 'im a big barrel, an' fill it half full er water fum de big springs. Den he piled up 'bout a cord er wood, an' ez he piled, he put rocks 'twix' de logs, an' den he sot de wood after at bofe een's an' in de middle. 'Twan't long 'fo' dey had de hogs killt, an' eve'ything ready fer ter scrape de ha'r off. Den he tuck de red-hot rocks what he put in de fire, an' flung um in de barrel whar de water wuz, an' 'twan't long, mon, 'fo' dat water wuz ready fer ter bile. Den dey tuck de hogs, one at a time, an' soused um in de water, an' time dey tuck um out, he ha'r wuz ready fer ter drap out by de roots. Den dey'd scrape un wid sticks an' chips, an' dey ain't leave a ha'r on um.

"Well, bimeby, dey had all de hogs killt an' cleaned, an' hauled off, an' when eve'ything wuz still ez a settin' hen,

ol' Brer Rabbit stuck his head out fum behine a bush whar he been settin' at. He stuck his head out, he did, an' look all 'roun', an' den he went whar de fier wuz an' try fer ter warm hisse'f. He ain't been dar long 'fo' here come Brer Wolf an' Brer Fox, an den he got busy.

"He say, 'Hello, frien's! howdy an' welcome! I 'm des fixin' fer ter take a warm baff like Mr. Man gi' his hogs; wont you j'ine me?' Dey say dey ain't in no hurry, but dey holp Brer Rabbit put de hot rocks in de barrel an' dey watch de water bubble, an' bimeby, when eve'ything wuz ready, who should walk up but ol' Mr. Lion?

"He had a mane fum his head plum ter de een' er his tail, an' in some places it wuz so long it drug on de groun'—dat what make all de creeturs 'fear'd un 'im. He growl an' ax um what dey doin', an' when Brer Rabbit tell 'im, he say dat's what he long been needin'. 'How does you git in?' 'Des back right in,' sez ol' Brer Rabbit, sezee, an' wid dat Mr. Lion backed in, an' de water wuz so hot, he try fer ter git out, an' he slipped in plum ter his shoulder-blades. You kin b'lieve me er not, but dat creetur wuz scall'd so dat he holler'd an' skeer'd eve'ybody fur miles aroun'.

"An when he come out, all de wool drap't out, 'cep' de bunch you see on his neck, an' de leetle bit you'll fin' on de een' er his tail—an' dat'd 'a' come off ef de tail hadn't 'a' slipped thoo de bung-hole er de barrel." With that, Uncle Remus closed his eyes, but not so tightly that he couldn't watch the little boy. For a moment the child said nothing, and then, "I must tell that tale to mother before I forget it!" So, saying, he ran out of the cabin as fast as his feet could carry him, leaving Uncle Remus shaking with laughter.

Brer Rabbit's Flying Trip

Brer Rabbit concocts so many pranks that those around him tire of his trickery and want to find a way to stop him. Brer Fox promises a pot of gold to whoever takes the job and Brer Buzzard volunteers. Buzzards have a wingspan of up to six feet. They are clumsy when flapping their wings unlike other birds, but are experts in soaring for long periods of time. In this case, Brer Buzzard is not only bad at wing-flapping, but he's also an old bird. Brer Rabbit appears before he is summoned and quickly expresses a desire to learn how to fly, meaning he wants to take a ride on the old bird's back. Brer Buzzard, like so many before him, learns that taking on Brer Rabbit is a difficult proposition.

Dar once wuz a time when most er de creeturs
Got mighty tired er Brer Rabbit's capers,
An' dey 'semble', dey did, grass an' meat eaters.
Browsers an' grazers, an' likewiss de bone-scrapers,
Fer ter see what dey kin do.

Brer B'ar wuz dar, wid his bid fur suit on,
An' ol' Brer Wolf fetched his big howl along,
An' when eve'ything wuz ready, wid a long, loud hoot on,
Here come ol' Simon Swamp Owl along,
A-tootin' of his too-whoo.

Dar wuz ol' Brer Fox, suh, wid his black socks, suh,
An' a heap er creeturs dat I don't hatter mention;
Some bow-legged an' some knock-kneed in de hocks, suh.
An' dey all agree fer ter hol' a convention
Fer ter stop Brer Rabbit's pranks.

Brer Fox, he 'low he'll gi' a pot er gol', suh,
Ter de man what kin tol Brer Rabbit off, suh;
Brer Buzzard say, "I'm a-gittin' ol', suh,
But I'll try my han'," an' den he cough, suh.
An' de rest un um bowed dere thanks.

Now, ol' Brer B'ar wuz a-settin' in de cheer, suh,
So, he stand up an' move a motion;
He up an' 'low, "Le's erso'v right here, suh,
Fer ter thank Brer Buzzard whiles we're in de notion,
An' not put it off ter some yuther day."

An' den dey had it up an' down, suh,
'Sputin' 'bout what dey oughter do,
Some wanter gi' 'im a flower crown, suh,
Ef he rid Brer Rabbit up dar in de blue,
An' drap 'im when he got half-way.

Dey sont a runner atter ol' Brer Rabbit
Ter ax 'im ter call an' 'ten' de convention;
But ol' frien' Wobble-nose had a quare habit
Er knowin' a thing befo' it wuz mention',
An he come 'fo' he got de word.

He wiggle his nose, an' wunk his eye—
"Here sho is de man I wants ter see, suh!
Brer Buzzard I'm tryin' ter l'arn how ter fly!"
An' c'ose Brer Buzzard gi' his agree, suh,
An' all un um say he's a 'commydatin' bird!

An' den Brer Buzzard half spread his wing, suh
He try ter look young, but he wuz ol' suh—
He try ter strut an' walk wid a swing, suh;
He wuz dreamin' 'bout dat pot er gol', suh,
An' what he wuz gwine fer ter buy.

Brer Buzzard ain't skacely got thoo wid his pride, suh,
'Fo' Brer Rabbit lit right 'tween his floppers,
Wid, "Now, hump yo'se'f, an' gi' me a ride, suh,
Ef you don't I'll hit—I'll hit you some whoppers
When I git you up dar in de sky!"

Well, de creeturs grinned when Brer Buzzard riz, suh.
An' made a big fuss accordin' ter der natur';
Ez fer ol' Brer Rabbit, de pleasure wuz all his, suh
De ridin' wuz easy ez eatin' tater
When it's b'iled an' made inter pie!

Kaze under bofe wings he had a paw, suh,
An', when Brer Buzzard try fer ter drap 'im.
He'd scratch an' tickle 'im wid his claw, suh;
An' when Brer Buzzard try fer ter flap 'im,
He'd scratch an' wink his eye!

An' wid his claws he tuck an' steered 'im
Fum post ter pillar in de deep blue, suh;
He'd holla an' laugh—all de creeturs heer'd 'im—
You know how you'd feel ef it hab been you, suh,
A-waitin' fer some un ter fall!

When ol' Brer Rabbit got tired er ridin',
He steered Brer Buzzard right straight ter de groun', suh,
An' den an' dar went right inter hidin'.
When de creeturs come up he couldn't be foun', suh,
An' I speck an' I reckon dat's all!

Brer Rabbit and the Gold Mine

*This story begins with a famine for almost everyone
except for Brer Rabbit and his family due to the fact
that he had previously fattened up and had some food
stored. As usual in cases such as this, the creatures
get together to decide what to do. Brer Rabbit tells
the other animals that there is a nearby gold mine,
but they are skeptical. Still, they start looking just in
case. Hunger can cause you to do irrational things.
Although Brer Wolf tries to trick Brer Rabbit, the
trickster doesn't take the bait.*

There had been silence in the cabin for a long ten minutes, and Uncle Remus, looking up, saw a threat of sleep in the little boy's eyes. Whereupon he plunged headlong into a story without a word of explanation.

"Well, suh, one year it fell out dat de craps wuz burnt up. A dry drouth had done de work, an' ef you'd 'a' struck a match anywhar in dat settlement, de whole county would 'a' blazed up. Ol' man Hongriness des natchally tuck of his cloze an' went paradin' 'bout eve'ywhar, an' de creeturs got bony an' skinny. Ol' Brer B'ar done better dan any un um, kaze all he hatter do wuz go ter sleep an' live off'n his own fat; an' Brer Rabbit an' his ol' 'oman had put some calamus root by, an' saved up some sugarcane dat dey fin' lyin' 'roun' loose, an' dey got 'long purty well. But de balance er de creeturs wuz dat ga'nt dat dey ain't got over it down ter dis day.

"De creeturs had der meetin' place, whar dey could all set 'roun' an' talk de kind er politics dey had, des like folks does at de crossroads grocery. One day, whiles dey wuz all settin' an' squottin' 'roun', jowerin' an' confabbin', Brer Rabbit, he up 'n' say, sezee, dat ol' Mammy-Bammy-Big-Money tol' his great gran'daddy dat dar wuz a mighty big an' fat gol' mine in deze parts, an' he say dat he wouldn't be 'tall 'stonished ef 'twant some'rs close ter Brer B'ar's house. Brer B'ar, he growled, he did, an' say dat de gol' mine better not let him fin' it, kaze atter he got done wid it, dey won't be no gol' mine dar.

"Some laughed, some grinned an' some gapped, an', atter jowerin' some mo', dey all put out ter whar der famblies wuz livin' at; but I boun' you dey ain't fergit 'bout dat gol' mine, kaze, fum dat time on, go whar you mought,

you'd ketch some er de creeturs diggin' an' grabblin' in de
groun', some in de fields, some in de woods, an' some in
de big road; an' dey wuz so weak an' hongry dat dey kin
skacely grabble fer fallin' down.

"Well, dis went on fer de longest, but bimeby, one
day, dey all 'gree dat sump'n bleeze ter be done, an' dey
say dey'll all take one big hunt fer de gol' mine, an' den
quit. Dey hunted in gangs, wid de gangs not fur fum one
an'er, an' it so happen dat Brer Rabbit wuz in de gang
wid Brer Wolf, an' he know'd dat he hatter keep his eyes
wide open. All de creeturs hatter dig in diffunt places, an'
whiles Brer Rabbit want much uv a grabbler, he had a way
er makin' de yuthers b'lieve dat he wuz de best er de lot.
So, he made a heap er motion like he wuz t'arin' up
de yeth.

"Dey ain't been gwine on dis away long fo' Brer Wolf
holler out, 'Run here, Brer Rabbit! I done foun' it!' Brer B'ar
an' Brer Fox wuz bofe diggin' close by, an' Brer Rabbit
kinder wunk one eye at de elements; he say, sezee, 'Glad I is
fer yo' sake, Brer Wolf; git yo' gol' an' 'joy yo'se'f!'

"Brer Wolf say, 'Come git some, Brer Rabbit! Come git some!'

"Ol' Brer Rabbit 'spon', 'I'll take de leavin's, Brer Wolf;
you take what you want, an' den when you done got 'nough
I'll get de leetle bit I want.'

"Brer Wolf say, 'I wanter show you sump'n.'

"Brer Rabbit 'low, 'My eyes ain't big fer nothin'.'

"Brer Wolf say, 'I got a secret I wanter tell you.'

"Brer Rabbit 'low, 'My y'ears ain't long fer nothin'. Des
stan' dar an' do yo' whisperin', Brer Wolf, an' I'll hear eve'y
word you say.'

"Brer Wolf ain't say nothin', but make out he's grabblin', an' den, all of a sudden, he made a dash at Brer Rabbit, but when he git whar Brer Rabbit wuz at, Brer Rabbit ain't dar no mo'; he done gone. Weak an' hongry ez he is, Brer Wolf know dat he can't ketch Brer Rabbit, an' so he holler out, 'Whar you gwine? 'Hat's yo' hurry, Brer Rabbit?'

"Brer Rabbit holler back, 'I'm gwine home atter a bag fer ter tote de gol' you gwine leave me! So long, Brer Wolf; I wish you mighty well!' an' wid dat he put out fer home."

How Brer Rabbit Got a House

This story is about the way Brer Rabbit decides he wants a house but doesn't want to build it himself. He tricks other creatures into building it for him and then manages to get the house all for himself. He uses mind games and trickery for getting things done without having to do any work himself. Much like the character of John in other African tales, Brer Rabbit constantly strives for one-upmanship, thereby mirroring the desires of the enslaved to acquire status and power.

Oh, once 'pon a time, all de creeturs, all de creeturs,
Tuck a notion dat dey'd build a house,
An' fix it so ez ter keep out de skeeters,
An' fix it up nix cummy rous!

Dey all wuz dar fum de B'ar ter de Possum,
Brer Wolf, Brer Fox, Brer Coon,
Wid ol' Brer Rabbit fer ter stan' 'roun' an' boss um,
Kaze dey hatter have de' house right soon.

Brer Rabbit, he wuz busy, oh, yes, mighty busy,
Not doin' uv a blessed thing;
Ef he clim' de scaffle, he say he'll git dizzy,
So he medjur an' mark an' sing.
Dey buil' de house, an' it sho wuz a fine un,
Made er poplar, oak an' pine;
De littlest room wuz a sev'm-by-nine un,
Whar de sick could go an' whine!

Brer Rabbit, he wait, an' when de time come,
He choosened a upsta's room,
An' dar he sot (ef I kin make de rhyme come)
A-singin' "Hark fum de Toom!"
An' den he got what he ain't had oughter,
Ez all de creeturs said,
A gun, a cannon, an' a tub er water,
An' hid um under his bed!

When de creeturs come home, Brer Rabbit wuz ready,
An' he tell um he gwineter set down;
"Well, set," sez dey, "an' we'll try ter be ste'dy,"
An' wid dat, Brer Rabbit kinder frown;
Bang-bang! went de gun—de barrels wuz double—
An' de creeturs wuz still ez mice;

Brer B'ar he say, "Dy must be some trouble,
But I hope heedon't loosen de j'is!"

Brer Rabbit, he say, "Wharbouts mus' I spit at?"
An' Brer Wolf answer, wid a grin,
"Des wharsomever you kin make it hit at!"
Brer Fox, he rub his chin;
Brer Rabbit, he tuck de tub er water,
An' empty it all on de sta'rs,
An' it come nigh drownin' Brer Coon's daughter.
An' likewise one er Brer B'ar's!

Brer Rabbit say, "When I sneeze I'll skeer you,
An' I hate fer ter have it ter do!"
Brer Fox say, "We'll lissen an' hear you,
Des go right ahead wid yo' sneeze-a-ma-roo!"
Boom-a-lam! went de cannon, an' de creeturs, dey lit out,
Thoo window-sash an' do',
Any way, any way dat dey kin git oot,
An' dey ain't come dar no mo'!

Brer Rabbit and the Partridge Nest

Like other Brer Rabbit tales, this one provided enslaved Africans with a way to navigate the deceitful system of slavery. Using trickery to gain some partridge eggs supplies Brer Rabbit with a food source and a way to survive another day. More importantly, his thievery gives him power. Brer Rabbit stories use allegory to demonstrate how the weak are able to obtain what they need by continuously finding ways to manipulate a situation while depriving others of their property and capabilities.

Oh, what's de matter wid de Whipperwill,
Dat she sets an' cries on de furder hill?
An' what's de matter wid Miss Bob White,
Dat she choke herse'f wid sayin' goodnight?
You know mighty well dat sump'n is wrong
When dey sets an' sings dat kinder song,
'Twix' a call an' a cry, 'twix' a weep an' a wail—
Dey must be tellin' a mighty sad tale.

Miss Whipperwill's troubles, an' what she say
Will do fer ter tell some yuther day;
But Miss Bob White—My! Ain't she a sight?—
I'll hatter tell why she hollers goodnight.
Dey once wuz a time (needer mo' ner less)
When she ain't try ter hide ner kivver her nes';

She built it in de open, whar all kin see,
An' wuz des ez perlite ez she kin be.
She'd make her house facin' eas' an' wes',
An' den wid eggs she'd fill her nes';
Fer ter keep um warm she'd brood an' set,
An' keep her house fum gittin' wet.
Whiles dis gwine on, Brer Rabbit come by,
A-wigglin' his mouf, an' a-blinkin' his eye:
"De top er de mornin', Miss Bob," sezee;
"De same ter you, Brer Rabbit," se' she.

Sez ol' Brer Rabbit, "I been missin' you long,
I wuz mighty fear'd dat sump'n wuz wrong,
But here you set ez still ez a mouse,
Not doin' nothin' but keepin' house!"
"Oh, well," se' she, "I'm too ol' ter gad,
I use' ter do it, but I wish I never had!
De only thing I want is ter wash my dress,
But I can't do dat whiles I'm on my nes'."

Brer Rabbit, he say, "Can't I he'p you out?
I ain't doin' nothin' but walkin' about,
An' my ol' 'oman is willin' fer ter bet
Dat ef settin's de thing, I'm ol' man set!"
"I know mighty well," sez Miss Bob White,
"Ef you set a-tall, it'll be done right."
"Thanky-do, Miss Bob! Go wash yo' dress,
An' I'll do what I kin fer ter kivver yo' nes'!"

So off she put, wid a flutter an' a flirt,
An' washed her dress in a pile er clean dirt;
Brer Rabbit see de eggs, an' shuck his head;
His mouf 'gun ter dribble, an' his eye turn red;
Sezee, "It'd sholy be hard fer ter match um,
So I'll des take um home an' try fer ter hatch um!"
So said, so done! An' den when he come back,
He come in a gait 'twix' a lope an' a rack.

An' Miss Bob White, atter washin' her dress,
Went a-runnin' back ter house an' nes';
"Much erbleege, Brer Rabbit," an' den she bowed.
"Say nothin', ma'am, fer ter make me proud,
Kaze I been a-waitin' here, frettin' an' sweatin',
Fer fear I ain't sech a good han' at settin';
My ol' 'oman say I got a slow fever,
An' I 'clar' ter goodness, I'm ready ter b'lieve her!

"I felt sump'n move, I hear' sump'n run,
An' de eggs done gone—dey ain't na'er one!
I sho is seed sights, I done hear folks talk—
But never befo' is I seed eggs walk!"
"My goodness, me!" sez Miss Bob White,
A-peepin' in de nes', "You sho is right!"
An' y'ever sence den, when darkness falls,
She gives de lost chillun her goodnight calls!
An' y'ever sence den, when darkness falls,
She gives de lost chillun her goodnight calls!

Brer Rabbit Gets Brer Fox a Hoss

Some animals love the water; others, like Brer Rabbit and Brer Fox, don't. At least they don't like wading in the river themselves. But they figure if they had a hoss (horse) they could ride the animal and enjoy being in the water. So, Brer Rabbit and Brer Fox decide to get themselves a hoss. Once again, the trickster hoodwinks Brer Fox by directing him to hold the hoss's tail. In doing so, Brer Rabbit enjoys a sideshow at the expense of a predatory foe.

Not many er de creeturs wuz fon' er water,
Onless it mought 'a' been Brer Coon's daughter;
Brer B'ar, Brer Fox, an' ol' Brer Rabbit,
Dey vow'd dey can't never git in de habit
Er wadin' de creek, er swimmin' de river—
When it come ter dat, dey'd run ter kivver!
When folks come 'long fer ter git across,
De creeturs tuck notice dat dey rid a hoss.

Brer Fox, he say he wish he had one,
An' 'mongst all de yuthers he'd be de glad un;
He'd git a bridle an' a bran' new saddle,
An' git on de hoss an' ride 'im straddle;
He say, sezee, "He'd do some trottin',
Kaze when I git started, I'm a mighty hot un!"
Brer Rabbit, he smole a great big smile,
Wid, "I can't ride myse'f, kaze I got a b'ile!

"But it seem like ter me dat I knows whar a hoss is:
He's away back yan' whar two roads crosses,
An' I'll meet you dar termorrer mornin',
Des 'bout de time when day's a-dawnin'.
"Brer Fox, he say, "I hear yo' sesso,
An' ef I ain't sick I'll be dar desso!"
Brer Rabbit tip his hat, wid, "So-long, frien';
We'll git de hoss, you may depen'."

Long 'fo' de time, Brer Rabbit wuz a-stirrin',
An' he chuckle ter hisse'f like a cat a-purrin';
De hoss wuz stretched out asleep in de pastur';
Brer Rabbit went up des ez close ez he dast ter,
Fer ter see ef he 'live: hoss switched his tail, suh!
"Dis time we'll git you widout fail, suh!"
So, Brer Rabbit say; den he seed Brer Fox—
"An' an'er fine gent fer ter git in a box!"

Den he say out loud, "Good luck done sont 'im,
An' laid 'im down right whar you want 'im!
Ef youer tied ter his tail, you kin sholy hol' 'im,
An' mo' dan dat, you kin trip 'im an' roll 'im!"
So said, so done! an' dar Brer Fox wuz,
Right close ter de place whar a heap er knocks wuz!
Brer Rabbit, he holla, "Hol' 'im down! Hol' 'im down!
Des make 'im stay right spang on de groun'!"
De hoss, he riz wid a snort an' a whicker,
An' showed dat he wuz sump'n uv a kicker!
An' den an' dar, Brer Rabbit 'gun ter snicker,
Wid, "Hol' 'im, Brer Fox! 'Twon't do ter flicker!

Ef you make 'im stan' still, you kin ride 'im de quicker!"
De hoss, he r'ar'd an' raise a mighty dust up,
An' fust thing you know, Brer Rabbit hear a bust-up!
"I hope, Brer Fox, dat you ain't much hurt—
But yo' wife'll be mad, kaze you done tored yo' shirt!"

Brer Rabbit Treats the Creeturs to a Race

This folktale starts out with Uncle Remus getting in the mood for a storytelling session with the little boy. In this story, Brer Rabbit, who is forever making plans for entertaining the other creatures, asks if Rainmaker can arrange a race between Brer Dust and Cousin Rain. All the creatures come to see the race, just as they do these days for a big race. But this race is not like any other, as the onlookers get caught up in the commotion.

One sultry summer day, while the little boy was playing not far from Uncle Remus's cabin, a heavy black cloud made its appearance in the west, and quickly obscured the sky. It sent a brisk gale before it, as if to clear the path of leaves and dust. Presently there was a blinding flash of lightning, a snap and a crash, and, with that, the child took to his heels and ran to Uncle Remus, who was standing in his door. "Dar now!" he exclaimed, before the echoes of the thunder had rolled away, "Dat dust an' win' an' rain. Puts me in mind er de time when ol' Brer Rabbit got up a big race fer ter pleasure de yuther creeturs. It wuz de mos' funniest race you ever hear tell on. Brer Rabbit went 'way off in de woods twel he come ter de Rainmaker's house. He knocked an' went in, an' he ax de Rainmaker ef he can't fix it up so dey kin have a race 'tween Brer Dust an' Cousin Rain, fer ter see which kin run de fastes'. De Rainmaker growled an' jowered, but bimeby he 'gree, but he say that ef 'twuz anybody but Brer Rabbit, he wouldn't gi' it but one thunk.

"Well, dey fix de day, dey did, an' den Brer Rabbit put out ter whar de creeturs wuz stayin' at, an' tol' um de news. Dey dunner how Brer Rabbit know, but dey all wanter see de race. Now, him an' de Rainmaker had fixt it up so dat de race would be right down de middle er de big road, an' when de day come, dar's whar he made de creeturs stan'—Brer B'ar at de bend er de road, Brer Wolf a leetle furder off, an' Brer Fox at a p'int whar de crossroads wuz. Brer Coon an' Brer Possum an' de yuthers be scattered about up an' down de Road.

"Ter dem what has ter wait, it seem like de sun stops an' all de clocks wid 'im. Brer B'ar done some growlin'; Brer Wolf some howlin' an' Brer Possum some laughin'; but atter while a cloud come up fum some'rs. 'Twant sech a big cloud, but Brer Rabbit know'd dat Cousin Rain wuz in dar 'long wid Uncle Win'. De cloud crope up, it did, twel it got right over de big road, an' den it kinder drapped down a leetle closer ter de groun'. It look like it kinder stop, like a buggy, fer Cousin Rain ter git out, so der'd be a fa'r start. Well, he got out, kaze de creeturs kin see 'im, an' den Uncle Win', he got out.

"An' den, gentermens! De race begun fer ter commence.

Uncle Win' hep'd um bofe; he had his bellows wid 'im, an' he blow'd it! Brer Dust got up fum whar he wuz a-layin' at, an' come down de road des a-whirlin'. He stricken ol' Brer B'ar fust, den Brer Wolf, an' den Brer Fox, an' atter dat, all de yuther creeturs, an' it come mighty nigh smifflicatin' um! Not never in all yo' born days is you y'ever heern sech coughin' an' sneezin', sech snortin' an' wheezin'! An' dey all look like dey wuz painted red. Brer B'ar sneeze so hard dat he hatter lay down in de road, an' Brer Dust come mighty nigh buryin' 'im, an' 'twuz de same wid de yuther creeturs—dey got der y'ears, der noses, an' der eyeses full.

"An' den Cousin Rain come 'long, a-pursuin' Brer Dust, an' he come mighty nigh drownin' um. He left um kivver'd wid mud, an' dey wuz wuss off dan befo'. It wuz de longest 'fo' dey kin git de mud out 'n der eyes an' y'ears, an' when dey git so dey kin see a leetle bit, dey tuck notice dat Brer Rabbit, stidder bein' full er mud, wuz ez dry ez a chip, ef not dryer.

"It make um so mad, dat dey all put out atter 'im, an' try der level best fer ter ketch, but ef dey wuz anything in de roun' worl' dat Brer Rabbit's got, it's soople foots, an' 'twant no time 'fo' de yuther creeturs can't see ha'r ner hide un 'im! All de same Brer Rabbit ain't bargain fer ter have two races de same day."

"But, Uncle Remus," said the little boy, "which beat, Brother Dust or Cousin Rain?"

The old man stirred uneasily in his chair and rubbed his chin with his hand. "Dey tells me," he responded cautiously, "dat when Cousin Rain can't see nothin' er Brother Dust, he thunk he am beat, but he holla out, 'Brer Dust, wharbouts is you?' an' Brer Dust he holla back, 'You'll hatter scuzen me; I fell down in de mud an' can't run no mo'!'"

The Tar Baby

In what is probably the most well-known and widely shared Brer Rabbit story, Brer Rabbit is caught drinking milk that doesn't belong to him. To punish him, Brer Fox places a tar baby (dark, thick liquid distilled from wood or coal fashioned in the shape of a small child) near the milk container to capture the trickster. Disturbed by the tar baby, Brer Rabbit strikes him and gets stuck. When Brer Fox threatens extreme punishment, Brer Rabbit uses the age-old trick of reverse psychology to get out of a tight spot. He tells his captor that the worst punishment he could possibly endure would be to be thrown into a briar patch, a place Brer Rabbit knows well. In fact, it is his safe haven where he raises his children. In African American folklore, it is a metaphor for a retreat and a home. It is the quarters for the enslaved, the woods, or wherever one feels the safest. Simultaneously, however, it is a thorny place for its native inhabitants, where grief and internal struggles also abide. The Briar Patch is now the name of various inns, restaurants, and bed-and-breakfasts. This simplified retelling refers to the characters as Rabbit and Fox and comes from Richard Dorson's American Negro Folktales. It is a combination of two older stories from Joel Chandler Harris: "The Wonderful Tar-Baby Story" and "How Mr. Rabbit Was Too Sharp for Mr. Fox."

There was a Rabbit and a Fox. So they was having what they call a house-raisin'. An' the Rabbit was s'posed to be a doctor. And they had milk in the spring. An' this here Rabbit, every once in a while, he'd work a little bit, and he'd holler "Whoooooooooo." Fox said, "Who is that?" "Somebody callin' me." Says, "What they want?" "Oh I don't know, I ain't goin' to see." "Oh yes," says, "youse a doctor, you'd better go and see." So he went on down to the spring, and got in this milk, and drink some of it, come on back. And when he got back the Fox says, "Who is it, what was it?" Says, "Just Started."

All right, went on, worked a little bit, and directly he says, "Whooooooooo." "Who is it, who is that now?" "Somebody else callin' me. I ain't goin' this time." Fox says, "Yeah you go ahead," says, "you got to go, youse a doctor." He went on, down the spring, and drink up this milk, part of it, 'bout half of it, come back. Fox says, "What his name?" "Half Gone." [Laughter]

He went on back and worked a little bit, directly he said, "Whooooooooo." Says, 'What is that now?" "Somebody else calling me." "Well, better go see." "No, I ain't going." "Yeah, you go ahead." So he went on down the spring and drink it all up, filled the jug with water. Kept on doing that till the Fox 'cided he would see what, who it was. He put him a tar baby down there.

So, Rabbit he come down there an' seed him sitting there, say, "What you doing here?" Tar baby didn't say nothin' to him. "Speak du'n ye, I'll knock you over." Tar baby just sit there, didn't say a word. He hauled off and slapped him with one foot. When he slapped him that foot stuck to him. He says, "Better turn me loose, I got another un here," says, "I'll kick you with this, I'll kick you over." So he kicked him with that foot and that un stuck. He says, "You better turn me loose," says, "I got another one here," says, "I'll hit ye, kick ye with hit," says, "I'll kick ye clear over." He kicked him with that un, and that un stuck. He says, "Better turn me loose," says, "I got a head here, if I'll butt ye, I'll but ye to pieces." So he butted him, and his head stuck. There he was, couldn't get loose.

Fox he come down the spring, "Mhm, I knowed I'd get ye, I knowed you was the one drinking up my milk." He took him loose, started to the house with him. Says, "I don't know what hardly to do with you," says, "I'm going to take ye to the house." Got up the road pretty good piece toward the house, an' there was a big thick briar patch there. He says, "I'm a good mind to throw you out there in them briars." Rabbit says, "Ohh Mr. Fox, please don't throw me out there in them briars." Says, "I'll get all scratched up and all tore up with them briars," says, "don't throw me out there." [Plaintive] "Yes, I is, you shut up. Throw you right out there in the middle of 'em." After a while he took the Rabbit you know, and th'owed him over in the briar patch, and the old Rabbit kicked up his heels, said, "Ohh ho, here's where I want to be, here's where I was bred and bo'n anyhow."

BEARING WITNESS

In African and African American folktales, characters frequently bear witness to the injustice around them. This genre of tale demonstrates ways of navigating this injustice, presenting humorous situations in which unjust rules are circumvented and malevolent rulers outwitted. Tales about bearing witness resonate into the modern day, posing timeless questions about the nature of justice and the society we live in. Who should rule, and how should they rule? When are rules necessary, and when do they become overbearing and unjust? How do we overcome oppression and strive toward equality? A significant subsection of this genre are John and Old Master tales, which traditionally served as an act of defiance and community building. These tales tell stories of a clever enslaved man named John who outwits his enslaver in complex, funny, and meaningful ways. These tales of outsmarting the oppressor provided humor and hope to enslaved African people during a time that often felt bleak and hopeless.

Big John Gives Old Master a Sign

*This story was collected in Florida in the late 1930s. It
dates from the time of slavery. Enslaved people used to tell
many stories about how they outsmarted their enslavers.
These tales kept them hopeful in a world that seemed
hopeless. Often, the wise enslaved person who was able
to outwit his enslaver was called Big John. Telling tales like
this one was, in a way, an act of defiance, as Big John is
able to reverse the circumstances of who is in control. Tales
about Big John told in the days of slavery were enhanced
by the response of the audience. In this manner, these
tales were communal activities. While this tale places the
focus on Big John's successful tactic of escape, we cannot
overlook the enslaver's inhumane mistreatment of Big
John. This story represents a sad reality for many enslaved
people and should serve to educate about a horrific
time in history so that these atrocities are never again
repeated. However its more graphic moments may not be
appropriate for all audiences.*

Old Master and Old Miss had no sooner gotten on the
train than Big John sent word to all the other slaves
on all the plantations around that Old Master and Old Miss
had gone to Philadelphia and wouldn't be back for three
weeks. Big John had been left in charge of everything.
"Come over to the Big House," he invited everyone. "We'll
have a great time."

While the invitation was being passed around, Big John told some of his friends to kill some of Old Master's hogs so they could feast on them.

That night, Big John put together a fine table full of lots of food. Everyone who could get a hold of white folks' clothes had them on that night. Big John opened up the entire house and took Old Master's big rocking chair and put it on top of Old Master's bed. Then he climbed up and sat down on it to call out the dance steps. He was sitting in his high seat with a box of Old Master's cigars under his arm and one in his mouth when he noticed a couple of poor white folks coming into the house.

"Take them poor folks out of here," he instructed. "Take them back to the kitchen and don't allow them up front again. We don't want anything out here but quality."

Big John didn't know that these same white folks were Old Master and Old Miss dressed up in rags with dirt on their faces. They had slipped back to see how he would behave while they were gone. Of course, they were not happy. They washed the dirt off their faces and came back up front where Big John was sitting.

"John," said Old Master. "After I trusted you with my place, you went and smoked up all my fine cigars, and killed all my hogs, and let all those slaves in my house to act like they were crazy. Now I'm going to take you out to the persimmon tree and hang you. You deserve to be hung, and that's what I'm going to do."

While Old Master was going to get the rope, Big John called his friend Ike to one side and said, "Ike, Old Master is going to take me out and hang me on the persimmon tree.

Now, I want you to hurry out to that tree and climb up into it. Take a box of matches with you, and every time you hear me ask God for a sign, you strike a match."

After a while, Old Master came back with the rope, and he led Big John out to the tree. He tied a noose in the rope and put it around Big John's neck. He threw the other end over a limb.

"I've got just one favor to ask of you," said Big John. "Let me pray before I die."

"All right," said Old Master, "but hurry up and get it over with, 'cause I've never been so anxious to hang anyone in my life."

So, Big John knelt down under the tree and prayed, "Oh Lord, if you mean for Master not to hang me, give me a sign."

When he said that, Ike struck a match, and Old Master saw it and began to shake. Big John kept on praying. "Oh Lord, if you mean to strike Old Master dead if he hangs me, give me a sign." Ike struck another match, and Old Master said, "Never mind, John. You've prayed enough. The hanging's off."

But Big John kept on praying. "Oh Lord, if you mean to put Old Master and all of his family to death tonight, give me a sign." This time Ike struck a whole handful of matches, and Old Master lit out from there as fast as he could run.

And that's how the slaves got free. Big John scared Old Master so bad that he ended slavery right then and there.

Morning Sunrise

There are times, even today, when the father in a family decides who his daughter should marry, and that is what we see play out in this story. Since this daughter, Morning Sunrise, is very beautiful, she has several suitors. Because her father has a hard time deciding on who should become his son-in-law, he makes a plan to find his daughter the best man possible. The right husband is found using an ingenious trick.

Aman in one of the villages had a very beautiful daughter. She was so lovely that people called her "Morning Sunrise." Every young man who saw her wanted to marry her. Three, in particular, were very anxious to have her for their wife. Her father found it difficult to decide among them. He determined to find out by a trick which of the three was most worthy of her.

He bade her lie down on her bed as if she were dead. He then sent the report of her death to each of the three lovers, asking them to come and help him with her funeral.

The messenger came first to "Wise Man." When he heard the message, he exclaimed, "What can this man mean? The girl is not my wife. I certainly will not pay any money for her funeral."

The messenger came next to the second man. His name was "Witty Man." The latter at once said, "Oh dear, no! I shall not pay any money for her funeral expenses.

Her father did not even let me know she was ill." So, he refused to go.

"Thinker," the third young man—when he received the message—at once got ready to start. "Certainly, I must go and mourn for Morning Sunrise," said he. "Had she lived, surely she would have been my wife." So, he took money with him and set out for her home.

When he reached it, her father called out, "Morning Sunrise, Morning Sunrise. Come here. This is your true husband."

That very day the betrothal took place, and soon after the wedding followed. Thinker and his beautiful wife lived very happily together.

The Swimming Contest

John and Old Master tales are stories about oppressed Black people who became heroes through courage and ingenuity. In "The Swimming Contest," John outwits the enslaver and a would-be opponent. As the folklorist Zora Neale Hurston (1891–1960) once wrote, "John was too smart for Ole Massa. He never got no beatin'!" There are several John tales where he appears to demonstrate unusual strength, which is just deception, but makes John seem far smarter and stronger than anyone else. In this case, he hoodwinks his enslaver and another white man. John tales were not often publicly recorded until African American folklorists, such as Hurston and J. Mason Brewer, began to document them.

This I never heard anywhere in my life before, except from this friend of mine, and it was the biggest lie I ever heard. Will Gray—he was married to my stepsister—told me that fifty years ago. How we laughed!

This master freed his slaves, but one slave didn't want to leave. The master and his wife were leaving on a ship—probably for the Old Country, since they were going away from this country. So, the slave stowed away, and when they got nearly to land, he began to call out, "Oh, Massie George, oh, Massie George." At first it sounded faint, and then it kept getting louder. They said, "That must be John," but they couldn't believe it. He slipped out and began

swimming toward the boat. So, they pulled him aboard, all dripping, and asked him how he got there. "Well, I swim all the way here; I wasn't going to let you leave me."

So, he went along with them, and his master was bragging about how he had the best swimmer in the world. There was a white swimmer parading around, and they made a date with him to have a contest. The day of the contest he was waiting on the beach, until finally the colored man came, puffing and making a lot of noise, with a cookstove and provisions on his back. He said, "Where's that white fellow who's goin' to swim with me?" (in a big voice).

The white man said, "Here I am" (in a little voice).

John said, "Man, ain't you carrying nothing to eat with you?"

He answered "No."

"Well, you'd better, for I'm a-fixing to stay." The white man ran away.

The Fight

In these three versions of a classic folktale about a fight, we learn a lesson about knowing how to outsmart an adversary. While the fight looks like a mismatch, one man figures out how to win before the battle even starts, thus avoiding violence and denying his enslaver entertainment at the expense of the enslaved.

I.

There was once two plantation owners down in Mississippi, Coker and Brian Dewies, and they each had a bad man. They met each other in the road and they was sitting on their horses talking about the hands they had on the farm. And one said he had the baddest man. The other said his man was the baddest, could whip everybody. So, they was going to have a fight, and bet their plantation against the other plantation—Coker against Brian Dewies. All the hands and the sharecroppers went in with the bet, and whichever badman won, his master would take over.

They set the fight for Saturday evening. Coker's bad man was a little bitty fellow. Brian's was a big burly cat, like a mule. Coker's man told him, "Boss, you go saddle up your best saddle horse you got there." He was supposed to saddle the horse, but now he's giving the orders, 'cause the boss got his stake up: his home, plantation, money, and everything. "And git the shovel and go down and dig his grave, out there where we're going to fight, 'cause I'm going to kill him. I'll be down soon as I take a bath, and shave, and get my shoes shined. Hitch the horse out there and comb his mane." He was particular—he done take over now. He came down with a red handkerchief tied round his neck, and a starched and ironed overall suit. People was there by the thousands, come to see the fight. That's the farmer's day, Saturday—everybody comes to town.

He got there fifteen minutes late. The big fellow was in training with a thousand-pound maul, throwing it up a quarter of a mile, and then a half a mile up in the air. Then he'd dig down about four feet to get it out of the ground. He was pulling the trees up, four foot into the ground, and throwing them outside to get the ring cleared off.

The little fellow tells his boss, "Have you dug his grave yet?"

His boss said, "No."

Coker's man told him, "Start digging right now, 'cause I'm going to kill him." He pulled his coat off, going to work out a little before the fight. He reached out and to get the maul, but he couldn't lift it. So he yelled up to the sky. "Saint Peter, move over, and tell Sister Mary to move out the way, and move baby Jesus."

So, this big fellow said, "It's a little too rough around here for me."

II.

Two men had slaves, one named Mike and the other named Peter. The men often met and discussed the strength of their slaves, how they were giants and so forth. One day, they made a bet on them and all their friends made bets. They appointed a day to fight in the town square. They built an enclosure in the town square so all the people could see them fight to a finish. On the day set, a great crowd gathered. One man had come in and, seeing the enclosure, but not knowing it was the place for the fight, carried his horse on in the enclosure and hitched him. So, when Mike and Peter went inside, the first thing Mike did was go to the horse that was saddled and pick him up and lifted him over the fence.

When Peter saw that he said, "No fight."

III.

In the South, they always have one strong colored guy on all the plantations. He's given a lot of consideration by the boss—usually he be foreman. Can put two or three of the others in his back pocket.

So, one plantation owner said to the other, "My colored guy can whip your guy."

The other boss said, "I'll be damned if he can." So, they signed up for a fight, them two farm owners. Each man went and told the tough-colored guy on his place that he got a fight coming up. Each tough guy went off to himself thinking, "I can't whip that bastard." Jim said, "I can't whip John," and John said, "I can't whip Jim." But back in the times of slavery, you couldn't back out. So they set a date for the fight.

So, the boss said to each colored guy, "What do you want for the fight? What are you going to wear?" Jim thought he'd make a display to frighten John. He asked his boss to make a link chain, about four feet long, with an iron stake at the end of it, to drive into the ground, and to put an iron ring in his nose. And he'll be scratching and licking up dirt when John comes, like a bull, and running back and forward on the chain. And his boss will be trying to keep him quiet. "Steady, steady there, Jim, whoa, just a few minutes."

When John's boss asked him what he wanted, he said, "Just give me Old Puss to ride down to the battling ground." He was quiet-like. Tough, but quiet. He was slow riding down—he had almost liked to be late and forfeit the bet. That was a great big day, a holiday, people from twenty miles around was there in their horse and buggy and ox teams. So, when he was late, his Missus got worried, and as soon as he came riding down, she went over to him. John saw Jim on the chain and he was studying how to scare him; he was already scared himself. He was thinking fast, working his brains. When his Missus came over, he knew she would say something pretty flip. He thought, *The minute she opens her mouth, I'll slap her.* Missus said very roughly, "What kept you? Why you so late?" John, he slapped her face. Jim pulled up the stake and ran, sold out, forfeited the fight.

So the loser, Jim's master, had to pay off John's boss the three or four thousand dollars they'd put in a bag. Still, John's boss got mad about his wife being slapped. He asked John, "What was the idea slapping my wife?"

"Well, Jim knowed if I slapped a white woman I'd a killed him, so he run."

Big Feet Contest

Using African American dialect, John tales are often referred to as "John and Old Master" or "John and Old Marster" stories. Folktales often exaggerate in order to boast prowess. In this John and Old Master tale, an enslaved individual tells an unbelievable but humorous story that makes fun of the enslavers' need to boast. Where these stories originated is unknown, but they no doubt began as tales for amusement in small groups of Africans. They were helpful in coping with enslavement as they provided levity.

During the times of slavery the Old Marsters would get together and brag about which of their slaves had the largest feet. And one of the Old Marsters said, "My slave's feet are larger than yours."

And the other said, "No, my slave's feet are longer than yours."

The other slave owner says, "Give me proof that your slave's feet are larger than mine."

This was his proof. He says, "Whenever I buy shoes for my slave, they come in separate boxes, and they send a pair of oars with them."

The other slave owner gave his proof. Said, "You know the five hundred acres I own? You know those field mice was on those five hundred acres?" Says, "John was plowing at one end of the five hundred acres, and I hollered, 'Field mouse.' And John raised his foot. And I said, 'Did you get him, John?'

"And he said, 'Yes, if he's anywhere in the field.'"

The Yearling

Enslaved Africans rarely got enough healthy food to eat. When the author, educator, and orator Booker T. Washington was young, his mother would wake him up late at night to eat chicken. No doubt it was stolen from the farm where his family was enslaved, but it helped keep the young boy in good shape. In this John and Old Master tale, a yearling goes missing and the enslaver wants a confession. He enlists Mr. Preacher to find the thief. As is often the case, John's response for the preacher presents a different perspective.

In the old days, the only things the slaves got good to eat is what they stole. Old Marster lost a yea'ling, and some of the preacher's members knowed its whereabouts. So, Old Marster told him to preach the hell out of the congregation that Sunday, so that whosoever stole the yea'ling would confess to having it.

The preacher got up and pronounced to the crowd, "Some of you have stole Old Marster's yea'ling. So, the best thing to do is to go to Old Marster and confess that you stole the yea'ling. And get it off right now. Because if you don't, come Judgment Day, the man that stole the Master's yea'ling will be there. Old Marster will be there too, the yea'ling will be there too—the yea'ling will be staring you in the face."

John gets up and says to the preacher, "Mr. Preacher, I understand you to say, come Judgment Day, the man that stole Old Marster's yea'ling will be there, Old Marster will be there, the yea'ling will be there, yea'ling will be staring you in the face."

Mr. Preacher says, "That's right."

John replied then, "Let Old Marster git his yea'ling on Judgment Day then that'll be time enough."

Dividing Souls

This is another John and Old Master tale about stolen food, in this case apples. The story takes place in a cemetery where a skeleton has some advice for John, who snitches on two enslaved people to the enslaver. But John mistakes what he heard and reports to the plantation owner that the Lord and the Devil were counting souls. While this story provides an important lesson, it includes a violent end for John which may not be appropriate for all audiences.

During the period of slavery time, Old Marster always kept one slave that would keep him posted on the others, so that he would know how to deal with them when they got unruly. This slave was walking around in the moonlight one night and he heard a noise coming from the cemetery. It was two slaves examining apples, which they had stolen from Old Marster's orchard. They couldn't count,

so they were exchanging 'em. "You take dis un and I'll take dat un. Dis un's yours, and dat un's mine."

So, this slave heard them, and he listened, and he ran back to Old Marster. And running, he fell over a skeleton head, and he spoke to the skeleton head. "What you doing here?"

And the skeleton head said, "Something got me here, will get you here."

So, he told Old Marster when he got to the house that the Devil and the Good Lord was in the cemetery counting out souls. "Dis un's yours and dat un's mine. Dis un's yours and dat un's mine."

Old Marster didn't believe him, but he went with him to the cemetery. And Old Marster told him, said, "Now if the Devil and the Good Lord ain't counting out souls, I'm going to cut your head off."

Sure enough, the slaves had gone and Old Marster didn't hear anything, and he cut John's head off. Then John's head fell beside the skeleton head. Then the head turned over and said, "I told you something that got me here would get you here. You talk too much."

That's one my daddy would tell us when we were talking too much.

The Talking Eggs: A Story from Louisiana

This is a story about a widow who has two daughters. One is loved and the other is abused. Blanche does all the housework while Rose sits back and does nothing to help. The situation changes when Blanche meets an old woman with magical powers at the well. Some parts of this tale read like the story of "Cinderella," but this tale not only rewards Blanche; it also takes Rose to task for her inability to do much of anything but inappropriately laugh. The eggs in this folktale signify new growth and life, but only for Blanche.

There was once a widow who had two daughters, one named Rose and the other Blanche.

Blanche was good and beautiful and gentle, but the mother cared nothing for her and gave her only hard words and harder blows; but she loved Rose as she loved the apple of her eye, because Rose was exactly like herself, coarse-looking, and with a bad temper and a sharp tongue.

Blanche was obliged to work all day, but Rose sat in a chair with folded hands as though she were a fine lady, with nothing in the world to do.

One day, the mother sent Blanche to the well for a bucket of water. When she came to the well, she saw an old woman sitting there. The woman was so very old that her nose and her chin met, and her cheeks were as wrinkled as a walnut.

"Good day to you, child," said the old woman.

"Good day, auntie," answered Blanche.

"Will you give me a drink of water?" asked the old woman.

"Gladly," said Blanche. She drew the bucket full of water, and tilted it so the old woman could drink, but the crone lifted the bucket in her two hands as though it were a feather and drank and drank till the water was all gone. Blanche had never seen any one drink so much; not a drop was left in the bucket.

"May heaven bless you!" said the old woman, and then she went on her way.

And now Blanche had to fill the bucket again, and it seemed as though her arms would break, she was so tired.

When she went home her mother struck her because she had tarried so long at the well. Her blows made Blanche weep. Rose laughed when she saw her crying.

The very next day the mother became angry over nothing and gave Blanche such a beating that the girl ran away into the woods; she would not stay in the house any longer. She ran on and on, deeper and deeper into the forest, and there, in the deepest part, she met the old woman she had seen beside the well.

"Where are you going, my child? And why are you weeping so bitterly?" asked the crone.

"I am weeping because my mother beat me," answered Blanche, "and now I have run away from her, and I do not know where to go."

"Then come with me," said the old woman. "I will give you a shelter and a bite to eat, and in return there is many a task you can do for me. Only, no matter what you may see as we journey along together, you must not laugh nor say anything about it."

Blanche promised she would not, and then she trudged away at the old woman's side.

After a while they came to a hedge so thick and wide and so set with thorns that Blanche did not see how they could pass it without being torn to pieces, but the old hag waved her staff, and the branches parted before them and left the path clear. Then, as they passed, the hedge closed together behind them.

Blanche wondered but said nothing.

A little farther on they saw two axes fighting together with no hand to hold them. That seemed a curious thing, but still Blanche said nothing.

Farther on were two arms that strove against each other without a sound. Still Blanche was silent.

Farther on again two heads fought, butting each other like goats. Blanche looked and stared but said no word. Then the heads called to her. "You are a good girl, Blanche. Heaven will reward you."

After that she and her companion came to the hut where the old woman lived. They went in, and the hag bade Blanche gather some sticks of wood and build a fire. Meanwhile she sat down beside the hearth and took off her head. She put it in her lap and began to comb her hair and twist it up.

Blanche was frightened, but she held her peace and built the fire as the old woman had directed. When it was burning, the old woman put back her head in place and told Blanche to look on the shelf behind the door. "There you will find a bone; put it on to boil for our dinners," said she.

Blanche found the bone and put it on to boil, though it seemed a poor dinner.

The old woman gave her a grain of rice and bade her grind it in the mortar. Blanche put the rice in the mortar and ground it with the pestle, and before she had been grinding two minutes the mortar was full of rice, enough for both of them and to spare.

When it was time for dinner, she looked in the pot and found it was full of good, fresh meat. She and the old woman had all they could eat.

After dinner was over the old woman laid down on the bed. "Oh, my back! Oh, my poor back! How it does ache," groaned she. "Come hither and rub it."

Blanche came over and uncovered the old crone's back, and she was surprised when she saw it; it was as hard and ridged as a turtle's. Still she said nothing but began to rub it. She rubbed and rubbed till the skin was all worn off her hand.

"That is good," said the old woman. "Now I feel better." She sat up and drew her clothes about her. Then she blew upon Blanche's hand, and at once it was as well as ever.

Blanche stayed with the old woman for three days and served her well; she neither asked questions nor spoke of what she saw.

At the end of that time her mistress said to her, "My child, you have now been with me for three days, and I can keep you here no longer. You have served me well, and you shall not lack your reward. Go to the chicken-house and look in the nests. You will find there a number of eggs. Take all that say to you, 'Take me,' but those that say, 'Do not take me,' you must not touch."

Blanche went out to the chicken-house and looked in the nests. There were ever so many eggs; some of them were large and beautiful and white and shining and so pretty that she longed to take them, but each time she stretched out her hand toward one it cried, "Do not take me." Then she did not touch it. There were also some small, brown, muddy-looking eggs, and these called to her, "Take me!" So those were the ones she took.

When she came back to the house the old woman looked to see which ones she had taken. "You have done what was right," said she, "and you will not regret it." She then showed Blanche a path by which she could return to her own home without having to pass through the thorn hedge.

"As you go, throw the eggs behind you," she said, "and you will see what you shall see. One thing I can tell you: your mother will be glad enough to have you home again after that."

Blanche thanked her for the eggs, though she did not think much of them, and started out. After she had gone a little way, she threw one of the eggs over her shoulder. It broke on the path, and a whole bucketful of gold poured out from it. Blanche had never seen so much gold in all her life before.

She gathered it up in her apron and went a little farther, and then she threw another egg over her shoulder. When it broke a whole bucketful of diamonds poured out over the path. They dazzled the eyes they were so bright and sparkling.

Blanche gathered them up, and went on farther, and threw another egg over her shoulder. Out from it came all sorts of fine clothes, embroidered and set all over with gems. Blanche put them on, and then she looked like the most beautiful princess that ever was seen.

She threw the last egg over her shoulder, and there stood a magnificent golden coach drawn by four white horses, and with coachman and footman all complete. Blanche stepped into the coach, and away they rolled to the door of her mother's house without her ever having to give an order or speak a word.

When her mother and sister heard the coach draw up at the door, they ran out to see who was coming. There sat Blanche in the coach, all dressed in fine clothes, and with her lap full of gold and diamonds.

Her mother welcomed her in and then began to question her as to how she had become so rich and fine. It did not take her long to learn the whole story.

Nothing would satisfy her mother except for Rose going out into the forest, finding the old woman, and convincing the old woman to take her home with her as a servant.

Rose grumbled and muttered, for she was a lazy girl and had no wish to work for anyone—whatever the reward— and she would rather have sat at home and dozed; but her mother pushed her out of the door, and so, she had to go.

She slouched along through the forest, and presently she met the old woman. "Will you take me home with you for a servant?" asked Rose.

"Come with me if you will," said the old woman, "but whatever you may see, do not laugh nor say anything about it."

"I am a great laugher," said Rose, and then she walked along with the old woman through the forest.

Presently they came to the thorn hedge, and it opened before them just as it had when Blanche had journeyed there. "That is a good thing," said Rose. "If it had not done that, not a step farther would I have gone."

Soon they came to the place where the axes were fighting. Rose looked and stared, and then she began to laugh.

A little later they came to where the arms were striving together, and at that Rose laughed harder still. But when she came to where the heads were butting each other, she laughed hardest of all. Then the heads opened their mouths and spoke to her. "Evil you are, and evil you will be, and no luck will come through your laughter."

Soon after, they arrived at the old woman's house. She pushed open the door, and they went in. The crone bade Rose gather sticks and build a fire; she herself sat down by the hearth, and took off her head, and began to comb and plait her hair.

Rose stood and looked and laughed. "What a stupid old woman you are," she said, "to take off your head to comb your hair!" And she laughed and laughed.

The old woman was very angry. Still she did not say anything. She put on her head and made up the fire herself. Rose would not do anything. She would not even put the pot on the fire. She was as lazy at the old woman's house as she was at home, and the old crone was obliged to do the work herself. At the end of three days she said to Rose. "Now you must go home, for you are of no use to anybody, and I will keep you here no longer."

"Very well," said Rose. "I am willing enough to go, but first pay me my wages."

"Very well," said the old woman. "I will pay you. Go out to the chicken-house and look for eggs. All the eggs that say, 'Take me,' you may have, but if they say, 'Do not take me,' then you must not touch them."

Rose went out to the chicken-house and hunted about and soon found the eggs. Some were large and beautiful and white, and of these she gathered up an apronful, though they cried to her ever so loudly, "Do not take me." Some of the eggs were small and ugly and brown. "Take me! Take me!" they cried.

"A pretty thing if I were to take you," she cried. "You are fit for nothing but to be thrown out on the hillside."

She did not return to the hut to thank the old woman or bid her goodbye, but set off for home the way she had come. When she reached the thorn thicket, it had closed together again. She had to force her way through, and the thorns scratched her face and hands and almost tore the clothes off her back. Still she comforted herself with the thought of all the riches she would get out of the eggs.

She went a little farther, and then she took the eggs out of her apron. "Now I will have a fine coach to travel in the rest of the way," said she, "and gay clothes and diamonds and money." She threw the eggs down in the path and they all broke at once. However, no clothes, nor jewels, nor fine coach, nor horses came out of them. Instead, snakes and toads sprang forth, and all sorts of filth that covered her up to her knees and bespattered her clothing.

Rose shrieked and ran, and the snakes and toads pursued her, spitting venom, and the filth rolled after her like a tide.

She reached her mother's house, burst open the door,

and ran in, closing it behind her. "Look what Blanche has brought on me," she sobbed. "This is all her fault."

The mother looked at her and saw the filth, and she was so angry she would not listen to a word Blanche said. She picked up a stick to beat her, but Blanche ran away out of the house and into the forest. She did not stop for her clothes or her jewels or anything.

She had not gone very far before she heard a noise behind her. She looked over her shoulder, and there was her golden coach rolling after her. Blanche waited until it caught up to her, and then she opened the door and stepped inside, and there were all her diamonds and gold lying in a heap. Her mother and Rose had not been able to keep any of them.

Blanche rode along for a long while, and then she came to a grand castle, and the king and queen of the country lived there. The coach drew up at the door, and everyone came running out to greet her. They thought she must be some great princess come to visit them, but Blanche told them she was not a princess, but only the daughter of a poor widow. She told them that all the fine things she had, had come out of some eggs an old woman had given her.

When the people heard this, they were very surprised. They took her in to see the king and queen, and the king and queen made her welcome. She told them her story, and they were so sorry for her that they declared she should live there with them always and be as a daughter to them.

So, Blanche became a grand lady, and after a while she was married to the prince, the son of the old king and queen, and she was beloved by all because she was so good and gentle.

But when Blanche's mother and sister heard of the good fortune that had come to her, and how she had become the bride of the prince, they were ready to burst with rage and spite. Moreover they turned quite green with envy, and green they may have remained to the end of their lives, for all that I know to the contrary.

Big Sixteen

This John and Old Master tale was collected by the folklorist Zora Neale Hurston. Here John is referred to as Big Sixteen due to the extraordinary size of his shoes. Emphasizing John's strength, he easily provides the plantation owner with his requests. Surprised by John's ability to accomplish difficult tasks, Old Master asks John to catch the Devil. John kills the Devil, who is portrayed as a loser. But when John dies, he can't get into heaven or hell. So his soul becomes a ball of fire burning inside him, much like a jack-o'-lantern, a symbol in Igbo culture representing restless spirits that haven't received proper burials and have nowhere to go but roam the earth.

Back in slavery time, Marster had a Negro named John. John was such they named him Big Sixteen. Marster told Big Sixteen one morning to go down in his pasture and ketch

him dat wild hawg and bring him to him. Big Sixteen run dat hawg down and brought him to him. Marster thought that wuz pretty good, so he thought he'd try him out again.

So next morning Marster wanted to put some new blocks under his house, and he had some twelve by twelves in his cow lot and tole Big Sixteen to go bring him one. Big Sixteen goes and puts dat twelve by twelve on his shoulder and brings it to the house.

Next morning, Ole Marster decided to try him again. He tole Big Sixteen to go ketch up all his chickens. Big Sixteen caught all dat was roosting in yard and tree. How many? Two thousand.

"That was all, John, I believe you can ketch de devil."

John tole him, "Yeah, Marster, I kin ketch him."

Next morning, Marster tole him to go ketch de devil.

John tole him, "All right, Marster. Gimmie a shovel and a ten eb hammer."

Marster gits him de shovel and de ten eb hammer and John walks out about two hundred yards in front of de house and commenced digging in de dirt, digging dis hole. Finally, he come to de devil's house and knocked on de door. De devil's wife ast him who was it and he told her Big Sixteen. He ast her was Jack de Devil dere and she said yes.

"Tell him I wants to see him."

Devil cracked de door and peeped out and John tapped him in de forehead wid dat hammer and kilt him. John run in and grabbed him up and threw him crost his shoulder and carried him back to Ole Marster. His Marster tole him say, "I don't want dat ugly thing. Take him back."

Big Sixteen took him back and threw him in dat same

hole dat he had dug and buried him. 'Bout two weeks later, Big Sixteen died and he went to hell. Devil's wife and chillun saw him comin' and de chillun begin to run and hide; de wife saw him coming so straight till she slammed de door herself. Big Sixteen walks up and knocks on de door and she ast who was it. He tole her Big Sixteen. She tole him. "Go way! Go back! We don't want you down here. You're too bad!."

Big Sixteen goes on back. He goes to heben. When he got to heben he knocked on de gates. They ast who was it. He says Big Sixteen. They says, "Go on way from here. We don't want you here. You're too bad."

It was nowhere else for Big Sixteen to go. He had to come back to de earth. His soul changed to a ball of fire. He is wandering round on de earth and they calls him Jack-o'-Lantern . . . but it's nobody but Big Sixteen.

Diddy-Wah-Diddy

Diddy-Wah-Diddy is the best known of the mythical places from African American folktales. The story was collected in the 1930s. What is described here could also be "the promised land" or "the land of milk and honey." Versions of this story can be found in many religious texts, including Christian, Buddhist, and Islamic ones.

Diddy-Wah-Diddy is a wonderful place to go. It's geography is that it is "way off somewhere." It is reached by a road that curves so much that a mule pulling a wagonload of feed can eat off the back of the wagon as he goes. It is a place of no-work and no-worry for people and beasts. It is a very restful place where even the curbstones are good sitting-chairs.

The food is even already cooked. If travelers get hungry, all they need to do is sit down on the curbstone and wait. Soon they will hear something hollering, "Eat me! Eat me! Eat me!" and a big baked chicken will come along with a knife and fork stuck in it. You can eat all you want. By the time you feel full of chicken, a big deep sweet potato pie will push and shove to get in front of you. A knife and fork will be stuck up in the middle so you can cut a piece off and eat to your heart's delight. Nobody can ever eat it all up. No matter how much you eat, it just grows that much faster.

They say, "Everyone would live in Diddy-Wah-Diddy if it wasn't so hard to find and so hard to get to even after you know the way." Everything is on a large scale there. Even the dogs can stand flat-footed and lick crumbs off heaven's tables.

The biggest man there is known as Moon-Regulator because he reaches up and starts and stops the moon at his convenience. That is why there are some dark nights when the moon does not shine at all. He does not feel like putting it out into the sky those nights.

Most folks believe this place exists. It sure is good to think about, anyway.

PEOPLE WITH UNUSUAL POWERS

In African American folklore, stories often center around supernatural elements and capabilities. These tales provided African Americans with the opportunity to imagine scenarios where they held unique advantages over their oppressors, creating a sense of optimism and empowerment within the community. These stories give the underdog powerful qualities, allowing them a fairer fight against their captors. By creating unique mystical strengths, African supernatural folklore evokes a sense of wonder and hope for Black listeners and readers. Each specific supernatural quality, such as shape-shifting and Hoodoo practices, offers relevant strengths to the life of the oppressed and enslaved who chose to embrace them, while others favored religious principles to guide them. For those Black characters who believe and practice Hoodoo, unusual powers allow them to overcome difficult journeys and evade being caught, a common threat in the life of those escaping oppression. Zora Neale Hurston contributed greatly to this genre of tale—a genre that encapsulates the creativity, humor, and determination of African storytellers.

Uncle Monday

Writer, folklorist, and anthropologist Zora Neale Hurston's hometown was Eatonville, Florida, and it was this historic town that inspired the creation of many of the characters for her short stories and books. She is best known for her novel Their Eyes Were Watching God, *published in 1937. She did folklore fieldwork in Florida in the 1920s and 1930s. This tale was collected in the 1930s and is still told in Central Florida today.*

In his native Africa, Uncle Monday was a big medicine man—a leader in the powerful crocodile cult of men who claimed brotherhood with the savage reptiles. Captured and brought to America as a slave, Uncle Monday soon escaped and made his way from South Carolina and Georgia down into the Native American territory of Florida. There he made strong medicine among the Seminoles and their friends from the West Indies. When the white men banded together to drive the Native Peoples ever deeper into the peninsula, Uncle Monday led the tribesmen in retaliation. They made a last, desperate stand on the shores of Lake Maitland, but were again defeated by superior arms and numbers.

Uncle Monday then let his remaining warriors into the dense woods around Blue Sink Lake. He told them the gods had revealed to him that further resistance to the white men would be useless. But Uncle Monday swore that he would never submit to slavery or death at the hands of the whites. He said he would change himself into an alligator and join his brother reptiles in the Blue Sink until the wars were over, then he would come forth from the lake and walk the land in peace.

So the tribe held a ceremony on the banks of the Blue Sink. As the men beat African and Indian rhythms on their drums, Uncle Monday danced. As he danced his face grew long and terrible, his arms and legs grew shorter, his skin grew thick and scaly, and his voice changed to thunder. From the Blue Sink came an answering roar of deep-throated bellows, and a thousand gators swept up from the lake in a double column. Uncle Monday was the biggest alligator of them all, and he marched majestically between their ranks and slid into the Blue Sink. With a mighty roar, all the other alligators plunged after him.

That's how Uncle Monday changed himself into an alligator. He still lives in the Blue Sink but, every now and then, he changes himself back into a man and walks through the land casting all sorts of spells on folks.

Not long ago, old Judy Bronson of nearby Maitland was bragging around that Uncle Monday wasn't no better Voudou doctor than what she was. She said she could not only undo any spell he cast, but she could throw it right back on him. When Uncle Monday heard about her bragging, all he said was, "The foolishness of tongues is higher than mountains."

Then one day, Judy asked her grandson to rig up a pole and dig some worms for her; she was going fishing down at the Blue Sink, even if the mosquitoes and redbugs did eat her old carcass up. Folks tried to get her not to go, because

Blue Sink is bottomless a few feet from shore; but Judy said she just had to go, and that's all there was to it. She got there at sundown and had no sooner got her hook baited and in the water than she felt the dark slipping up and grabbing hold of her like a varmint.

Judy wanted to get up and run off through the brush, but her legs were paralyzed. Then she heard a big wind coming rushing across the brush, and the next thing she knew, she had fallen into the Blue Sink. Of all things on earth, Judy was most afraid of the dark and the water, and now they both had her in their claws. She was afraid to move for fear she might slip off into the deep. Finally, she found strength enough to scream, and at the sound of her voice, a bright beam of light fell across the Blue Sink like a flaming sword, pointing straight at her.

Then Judy saw Uncle Monday. He was clad in flowing robes and marching across the water toward her. Behind him swam an army of gators.

"I brought you here," said Uncle Monday, "and here you will stay until you own up that you can't do no such magic as me."

The light faded, and Uncle Monday and the gators sank beneath the water. But one big gator remained, and settled up so close to Judy she couldn't help touching him when she breathed.

Judy hated like everything to give way to Uncle Monday, but she was too scared to let pride stand in her way. First, she admitted it inside, and then she said it out loud. When she did, the alligator swam off into the darkness, and she heard her grandson calling to her. Soon, she was lifted out of the Blue Sink and carried home.

Folks still try to tell Judy that she only suffered a stroke and fell in the lake, but she knows better. She threw away all her Voudou potions, bottles, and equipment. She now says she has Uncle Monday to thank for being able to walk again. And she never questions Uncle Monday's medicine.

Such is the living power of Uncle Monday in the land around the Blue Sink. Sometimes, he walks through the countryside as a man, but he always changes into an alligator again and returns to the Blue Sink. When he does, all the other alligators in the lake keep up an all-night bellowing, and folks in the village hear them and breathe a sigh of relief. You see, both the alligators and the people living around Blue Sink feel much more comfortable with Uncle Monday home in the waters with his reptile family.

Railroad Bill

In many African American stories, Black people are depicted as being adept at moving through the landscape, a skill that is often needed when on the run. In this legend, Railroad Bill is not only able to escape being caught by knowing how and where to hide, he is able to change into an animal or a tree in order to elude the sheriff and his men. In storytelling, giving the underdog certain powers makes for a more even playing field and gives the character a chance to win at the game. It is fitting that Bill has the power to change into a fox, which is a sly and cunning creature. Railroad Bill is a folk outlaw. Our most famous Robin Hood-like outlaws are usually advocates for their communities, as is the case here. Railroad Bill, like many other outlaws, steals from the rich and gives to the poor. These characters are often forced into hiding by an injustice or minor crime, and they kill only in self-defense or to even the score.

An elderly Black woman opened the door of her unpainted shack, which was set back from the sandy road leading to Piney Grove near the Florida-Alabama line. On one of the splintered steps of the porch she found a stack of canned goods. She knew Railroad Bill had put them there during the night. She also knew they were stolen from an L&N boxcar. The woman understood that Bill should not have taken the canned goods, but she was mighty hungry. Without these canned foods, she would not eat.

The Escambia County sheriff had been chasing Bill for five years, but he would always escape. One time, the sheriff and his men took a train to a place where they thought Bill was hiding, but the elusive thief stayed in another car on the same train and loaded his sack with more plunder.

On another occasion, the sheriff's men followed Bill to an area where they had not searched before. When the hunters looked in a cluster of bushes, they chased a red fox from its hiding place. They shot, but the little red fox turned around and laughed at them in a high, wild, hearty roar. The old Black woman knew the fox was Railroad Bill. He had a way of turning himself into an animal or a tree.

The five-year chase leading to the arrest of Railroad Bill started shortly after the War Between the States when a man the white folks knew as Morris Slater refused to register the rifle he carried while hunting. Slater, a Black man, was then living in Bluff Springs where he worked for Bradford's Turpentine Company. When the sheriff had accosted Slater and told him to register the gun, Slater quickly walked away. One of the men shot at him but missed. Slater found shelter in a swamp near the railroad tracks. In order to survive, he robbed trains. The L&N officials in Montgomery hired detectives to track down the man who was now thought of as dangerous. He had exchanged shots with a railroad flagman and had also killed an Alabama lawman.

The hunt continued. Sheriff McMillan led a party to Bluff Springs. Railroad Bill, hiding behind a tree, saw the party coming and promptly shot the sheriff. One of the sheriff's

men fired several rounds at the Black man and thought he had killed the elusive Bill. Not wishing to retrieve the Black man's body at night, the sheriff's men left the scene. Next morning there was no sign of Railroad Bill—only the tree where he had been.

Bill finally met his end in Atmore, Alabama. The well-built bandit was sitting on a barrel eating crackers and cheese when Constable McGowan shot and killed him. When the body was searched authorities found his Winchester rifle concealed in the left pant leg and a loaded pistol in the belt. Railroad Bill's body was laid out on a packing crate. Bitterweeds were placed in his mouth.

His legend continues. African American folk songs about Bill were composed and passed on to the next generation. Many Blacks did not believe he was dead. When the federal government sent food commodities into the area during the Great Depression, many people believed the spirit of Railroad Bill had sent them.

A Ghost Story About an Aunt

The Federal Writers Project put many out-of-work folklorists and writers to work in the 1930s and 1940s. They collected a variety of stories throughout Florida. This one is based on a story tape-recorded by Robert Cook and Stetson Kennedy in January 1940. It is found in the Folklore Archives in the Library of Congress. Eartha White, who lived in Jacksonville, told it with the kind of enjoyment her mother must have passed onto her. While this story is about a ghost, it is not as frightening as many ghost stories are. This humorous tale invites speculation.

This is a true story my mother liked to tell. During the days of slavery, my mother was a house girl on a plantation on Amelia Island, which is off Florida's east coast near the Georgia border. She was born there. It is about an event she witnessed since she was there when it happened. This was an actual incident that took place sometime before the Civil War.

While dinner was being served, in the early evening, one of the family members raced home in such a panic he almost fell off his horse. He ran into the house and fell onto the floor. He startled everybody. When he calmed down and came to be more like himself, he began to tell about an experience he had just had on the road.

He said that as he was coming down the big road, just as he got near the cemetery, his aunt stopped his horse, which she had owned during her lifetime. She had passed away some time before, but there she was.

At first, the horse seemed to recognize her voice, and it stood at attention. But the man said that when he heard his aunt speak, every strand of his hair stood on end. And then he heard someone stroking the horse. And she said to the man, calling him by name, "Don't be afraid." She said, "I want you to meet me tomorrow, at sundown." And then she told him exactly where she would be. She continued, "I have something for you. I am your aunt. Meet me tomorrow at sundown. I am your aunt. I have something for you."

Right when she finished talking, the horse spooked and the man became more afraid than ever. So he ran home, stumbled up the steps, and fell into the dining room. He frightened everyone else with the look on his face and the panic in his voice. And when he calmed down, they said to him, "Certainly, you are going to meet her, hear what she has to say, and get whatever it is she has to give you?"

But the man, startled by his family's response, replied, "Not me! She can keep whatever it is she has. I won't be there!"

This is a real story, and my mother always delighted in repeating it.

The Tail of the Princess Elephant

Journeys by African Americans are not on equal par to white people's journeys due to historic and present discrimination including slavery, segregation, and unequal imprisonment. A Black storyteller need not be specific about the roadblocks and how to gain power, but it often includes magic. A bold imagination can help a man or woman find ways out of difficult situations, at least until someone else more cunning appears. Shape-shifting provides an advantage as do Hoodoo practices, which, in this tale, are associated with juju. African Americans often kept their juju charms in mojo bags, but in this case the young man named Kwesi keeps it hidden in his hair.

There once lived a woman who had three sons. These sons were very attached to their mother and always tried to please her. She at last grew very old and feeble. The three sons began to think about what they could do to give her great pleasure. The eldest promised that when she was dead, he would cut a fine monument in stone for her. The second said he would make her a beautiful coffin. The youngest said, "I will go and get the tail of the princess elephant and put it in the coffin with her." This promise was by far the hardest one to keep.

Soon after this, their mother died. The youngest son immediately set out on his search, not knowing in the least where he would likely find the tail. He traveled for three weeks, and at the end of that time he came to a little village. There he met an old woman, who seemed very surprised to see him. She said no human creature had ever been there before. The boy told the tale of his search for the princess elephant. The old woman replied that this village was the home of all the elephants, and the princess slept there every night. But she warned him that if the animals saw him, they would kill him. The young man begged her to hide him— which she did, in a great pile of wood.

She also told him that when the elephants were all asleep, he must get up and go to the eastern corner. There he would find the princess. He must walk boldly over, cut off the tail, and return in the same manner. If he were to walk stealthily, the elephants would waken and seize him.

The animals returned as it was growing dark. They said at once that they smelt a human being. The old woman assured them that they were mistaken. Their supper was ready, so they ate it and went to bed.

In the middle of the night, the young man got up and walked boldly across to where the princess slept. He cut off the tail and returned as he had come. He then started for home, carrying the tail very carefully.

When daylight came, the elephants awoke. One said he had dreamed that the princess's tail was stolen. The others beat him for thinking such a thing. A second said he also had had the dream, and he also was beaten. The wisest of the elephants then suggested that they might do well to go and see if the dreams were true. This they did. They found the princess fast asleep and quite ignorant of the loss of her tail. They wakened her and all started off in pursuit of the young man.

They traveled so quickly that in a few hours they came in sight of him. He was afraid when he saw them coming and cried out to his favorite idol, or juju, which he always carried in his hair, "O my juju Depor! What shall I do?" The juju advised him to throw the branch of a tree over his shoulder. This he did and it immediately grew up into a huge tree, which blocked the path of the elephants. They stopped and began to eat up the tree, which took them some little time.

Then they continued on their way again. Again the young man cried, "O my juju Depor! What shall I do?"

"Throw that corncob behind you," answered the juju. The lad did so, and the corncob immediately grew into a large field of maize.

The elephants ate their way through the maize, but when they arrived at the other side, they found that the boy had reached home. They had to give up the chase and return to their village. The princess, however, refused to do so, saying, "I will return when I have punished this impudent fellow."

She thereupon changed herself into a very beautiful maiden, and taking a calabash cymbal in her hand, she approached the village. All the people came out to admire this lovely girl.

She had it proclaimed through the village that whoever succeeded in shooting an arrow at the cymbal should have her for a bride. The young men all tried and failed. An old man standing by said, "If only Kwesi—the cutter of the princess elephant's tail—were here, he could hit the cymbal."

"Then Kwesi is the man I will marry," replied the maiden, "whether he hits the cymbal or not."

Kwesi was quickly fetched from the field where he was ploughing and told of his good luck. He, however, was not at all delighted to hear of it, as he suspected the maiden of some trick.

However, he came and shot an arrow which struck the center of the cymbal. The damsel and he were accordingly married—she preparing to punish him the entire time.

The night following their marriage, she turned into an elephant while Kwesi was asleep. She then prepared to kill him, but Kwesi awoke in time. He called, "O my juju Depor! Save me!" The juju turned him into a grass mat lying on the bed and the princess could not find him. She was annoyed, and next morning asked him where he had been all night. "While you were an elephant, I was the mat you lay on," replied Kwesi. The damsel took all the mats from the bed and burned them.

The next night the princess again became an elephant and prepared to kill her husband. This time the juju changed him into a needle and his wife could not find him. She again asked him in the morning where he had been. Hearing that the juju had helped him again, she determined to get hold of the idol and destroy it.

The next day, Kwesi was going again to his farm to plough a field. He told his wife to bring him some food to where he took his breaks. This time she was fairly certain that he could not escape. When he had had his food she said, "Now lay your head in my lap and sleep." Kwesi quite forgot that his juju was hidden in his hair and did as she bid. As soon as he was asleep, she took the juju out of his hair and threw it into a great fire which she had prepared.

Kwesi awoke to find her an elephant once more. In great fear he cried out, "O my juju Depor! What am I to do?" All the answer he got came from the flames. "I am burning, I am burning, I am burning." Kwesi called again for help and the juju replied, "Lift up your arms as if you were flying." He did so and turned into a hawk.

That is the reason why hawks are so often seen flying in the smoke of fires. They are looking for their lost juju.

How a Hoodoo Doctor Works

Hoodoo is used both as a noun referring to Southern African American magical practices and as a verb meaning to cast a spell or place a hex on someone. Here, Hoodoo is employed as root work practice. The root used in this root practice is High John the Conqueror, which can be used in varying ways, like being made into perfume or fashioned into a charm. All John the Conqueror roots are potent and provide protection. In this tale, Uncle John gives a suffering girl butterfly root tea that causes her to vomit. This distracts onlookers from his trickery with a lizard in a cup of boiled High John the Conqueror root. This protective root appears in numerous narratives of former enslaved people.

Years back they called it conju'ing; nowadays they call it Hoodoo.

Uncle John was the great Hoodoo doctor in times of slavery in the Deep South. Well, Uncle Bill's daughter Hannah got sick, so they sent for Uncle John, the doctor. He came and examined her, and he told her that she'd been conju'ed. Someone had put lizards in her, and they were alive. "But I'll be back on the morrow, and I'll get the lizards outta her." The news spread like wildfire that the doc would be back on the morrow to get the lizards out of Uncle Bill's daughter.

Uncle John always carried a greasy sack across his shoulder with a strap on the side, which was his medicine kit. So he goes through the woods, till he finds him a weed they calls a butterfly weed. He pulls it up and gets the root and puts it in his sack. Then he looked off to his right—there was a bush where John the Conquer growed up. He pulls that up too and gets the root of it in the sack. He walks a little farther, down to the edge of the water where it was damp, sees a log, and turns it over. "Here's what I'm looking for." He finds there was a lizard about four inches long and with four legs. He was shiny and spotted. He wraps him up in paper and drops him in the sack. Now this lizard is not poisonous and will not bite; he's awful harmless, and Doc knew it.

The girl was screaming and hollering that she could feel something crawling in her stomach. The peoples had gathered excited around the bed. In walked Doc, stepping quick and lively. "Git two cups quick as you can, put water in 'em, get 'em hot." He yet keeps his sack on his back, he never takes it off—as doctors do now, you know. Men begin to cut wood to start the fire. The women begin to put on the water. Doc, he reaches in his sack; he drops the butterfly root in one cup of hot boiling water, drops John the Conquer in the next one. In a few minutes they were both boiling. "Now I'll have to put everyone out the room except the mother and father—it's too exciting for you all to see."

He pours a big cup of butterfly root tea and gives it to her. She begins to scream, "Oh, Doc, I wants to heave, I wants to heave."

He said, "Hold her hand, rub her neck, be sure you got your hand rubbing right back of her neck. Mother, you rub her leg, just rub her leg right on the muscle; you ain't got time to look nowhere else but just where I told you to look at." Whiles they were holding her head, he eased his hand in the sack, gets a lizard, and dropped him in the bucket she was heaving into. He says, "Let her legs go, and run and get me a cup of John de Conquer right quick."

Hannah's mother ran and got the tea. "Here it is, Doc."

Doc says to Hannah, "Drink her down, drink her down."

After she had dranken it down, he told her, "I think I got that lizard." She got it easy. Doc said, "Let the peoples in now. I think I got that lizard. I don't know, but I think I got it." So, the peoples come in all excited to look at the girl, but she was at ease laying there quiet. They were really astonished. Doc says, "Hand me that stick there; I think I got that lizard—I don't know but I think I have." So, he begins to stir the bucket with the stick. Then the lizard starts to move. He says, "Oh, yes, I got it; here it is. Now bring me a pan and some cold water. I wants to be sure what it is."

They ran and brought him the water and the pan.

"One of you hand me another stick over there." So, they hand him another stick. That made him have two. He reached down in the bucket, and begins to stir again. The lizard begins to move. Doc grabbed him with the two sticks, lifted up the lizard, and put him into the pan of clear water.

Everybody was excited: "It's a ground lizard, it's a ground lizard." Doc says, "Give me a rag." He reaches in the pan with his hand and gets the lizard, rolls it up in the rag and puts it in the sack. Says, "I'll fix the Hoodoo that did her this work. He'll never conjure no one else." And Hannah, she was well from that day on.

Ògún and Aerosol Art

As the patron of ironwork in the Santería religion, Ògún is a powerful deity in the pantheon of orishas, which are immaterial spirits found in the Yoruba tradition. Each orisha is connected with an element found in the natural and human realm. As one of the first and most important orishas, Ògún used his machete to clear a pathway through the thick vegetation that covered the earth so that other orishas could descend from above. Ògún represents knives, machetes, hammers, axes, rakes, spades, hoes, and keys. This warrior spirit is the patron of blacksmiths, butchers, and metalworkers, as well as those who drive vehicles and work on the railroad. This tale represents the protective powers he employs on his followers. In this tale, an

artist shares his encounter with the deity and how Ògún has kept him safe while he creates his art along train tracks.

Ògún rules anything that is steel or iron—be it knives, bullets, guns, anything metallic, spray cans. You cannot run on train tracks without dealing with Ògún in one way or another.

One time I went with my mother to a *tambor*, a Santería celebration where people go into trances, they speak in tongues, they get possessed by deities. At one of these, Ògún comes down, points me out in the crowd, and says that I must wear his emblem, which is an iron chain link anklet on my right ankle. He told me, "If you run in my domain [the train track], you must wear this anklet." That came out of the clear blue sky, I did not know that person, or anyone else in that ceremony. It was very impressive, and the next day I had that anklet...

I had a lot of accidents on the train tracks from being electrocuted, falling off a catwalk, to getting hit over the head with a pistol by a police officer; many things that could have killed a lot of people...

But Ògún saved my ass many times while I was on the train tracks.

The Ballad of John Henry

Sometimes folktales, like this one, become so popular that they are made into ballads, plays, films, and books. This ballad tells the story of John Henry who is viewed as an American hero. Known as a "steel-driving man," he is credited for his work constructing a railroad tunnel. Grounded in a true story, Henry was so strong that he believed he could race against a steam-powered rock drill. As with many legends, the stories vary and are up for debate. Some say the event took place at Big Bend Mountain near Talcott, West Virginia. Others say it happened in the Lewis Tunnel in Virginia or in Alabama's Coosa Mountain Tunnel. This "man against machine" legend usually ends with John Henry's death while other tales have him walking away in triumph while dying later from exhaustion.

Well, every Monday morning,
When the bluebird begins to sing,
You can hear those hammers a mile or more,
You can hear John Henry's hammer ring, oh Lordy,
Hear John Henry's hammer ring.

John Henry told his old lady,
"Will you fix my supper soon?
Got ninety miles of track I've got to line,
Got to line it by the light of the moon, oh Lordy,
Line it by the light of the moon."

John Henry had a little baby,
He could hold him out in his hand.
Well, the last word I heard that poor child said:
"My dad is a steel-drivin' man, oh Lordy,
Daddy is a steel-drivin' man."

John Henry told his old captain,
Said, "A man ain't nothing but a man.
Before I let your steel gang down,
I'll die with the hammer in my hand, oh Lordy,
Die with the hammer in my hand."

John Henry told his captain,
"Next time you go to town
Just bring me back a ten-pound maul
For to beat your steel-drivin' down, oh Lordy,
Beat your steel-drivin' down."

John Henry had a old lady,
And her name was Polly Ann,
John Henry took sick and he had to go to bed,
Polly drove steel like a man, oh Lordy,
She drove steel like a man.

John Henry had a old lady,
And the dress she wore was red.
Well, she started up the track and she never looked back,
"Goin' where my man fell dead, oh Lordy,
Where my man fell dead."

Well, they taken John Henry to Washington,
And they buried him in the sand.
There was people from the East, there's people from
    the West,
Come to see such a steel-drivin' man, oh Lordy,
See such a steel-drivin' man.

Well, some said he's from England,
And some say he's from Spain,
But I say he nothin' but a Lous'ana man,
Just the leader of the steel-drivin' gang, oh Lordy,
Leader of the steel-drivin' gang.

Farmer Mybrow and the Fairies

*In African folklore, fairies signify a strong relationship
between humans, nature, and the spiritual world. They are
often the defenders of sacred places and have the power
to bring messages from one world to another. In this tale,
with the help of a group of fairies, Farmer Mybrow creates
a magnificent field of corn and yams—enough to feed a
great many people. But breaking promises with the fairies
is not advised. Nor is treating them with disrespect.*

Farmer Mybrow was one day looking about for a suitable
piece of land to convert into a field. He wished to grow
corn and yams. He discovered a fine spot, close to a great
forest which was the home of some fairies. He set to work at
once to prepare the field.

Having sharpened his great knife, he began to cut down
the bushes. No sooner had he touched one than he heard a
voice say, "Who is there, cutting down the bushes?"

Mybrow was too astonished to answer. The question
was repeated. This time the farmer realized that it must be
one of the fairies, and so replied, "I am Mybrow, come to
prepare a field."

Fortunately for him the fairies were in great good humor.
He heard one say, "Let us all help Farmer Mybrow to cut
down the bushes." The rest agreed. To Mybrow's great
delight, the bushes were all rapidly cut down—with very little
trouble on his part. He returned home, exceedingly pleased

with his day's work, having resolved to keep the field a secret even from his wife.

Early in January, when it was time to burn the dry bush, he set off to his field one afternoon with the means of making a fire. Hoping to have the fairies' assistance once more, he intentionally struck the trunk of a tree as he passed. Immediately came the question, "Who is there, striking the stumps?"

He promptly replied, "I am Mybrow, come to burn down the bush." Accordingly, the dried bushes were all burned down, and the field left clear in less time than it takes to tell it.

Next day the same thing happened. Mybrow came to chop up the stumps for firewood and clear the field for digging. In a very short time, his bundles of firewood were piled ready, while the field was bare.

So it went on. The field was divided into two parts—one for maize and one for yams. In all the preparations— digging, sowing, planting—the fairies gave great assistance. Still, the farmer had managed to keep the whereabouts of his field a secret from his wife and neighbors.

The soil, having been so carefully prepared, promised an exceedingly well harvest of crops. Mybrow visited the crops from time to time and congratulated himself on the splendid harvest he would have.

One day, while maize and yams were still in their green and milky state, Mybrow's wife came to him. She wished to know where his field lay, that she might go and fetch some of the firewood from it. At first, he refused to tell her.

However, she persisted, and finally succeeded in obtaining the information—but on one condition. She must not answer any question that should be of asked her. This she readily promised and set off for the field.

When she arrived there, she was utterly amazed at the wealth of the corn and yams. She had never seen such magnificent crops. The maize looked most tempting—being still in the milky state—so she plucked an ear. While doing so she heard a voice say, "Who is there, breaking the corn?"

"Who dares ask me such a question?" she replied angrily—quite forgetting her husband's command. Going to the field of yams, she plucked one of them also.

"Who is there, picking the yams?" came the question again.

"It is I, Mybrow's wife. This is my husband's field, and I have a right to pick." Out came the fairies.

"Let us all help Mybrow's wife to pluck her corn and yams," said they. Before the frightened woman could say a word, the fairies had all set to work with a will, and the corn and yams lay useless on the ground. Being all green and unripe, the harvest was now utterly spoiled. The farmer's wife wept bitterly, but to no purpose. She returned slowly home, not knowing what to say to her husband about such a terrible catastrophe. She decided to keep silent on the matter.

Accordingly, next day the poor man set off gleefully to his field to see how his fine crops were going on. His anger and dismay may be imagined when he saw his field a complete ruin. All his work and foresight had been absolutely destroyed through his wife's forgetfulness of her promise.

The Mermaid

All folktales have different variations that change over time and place, as demonstrated in these three mermaid stories. Mermaids are female; they are half human and half fish, have long hair, and these wear purple lipstick. While they are sometimes helpful and are associated with the sacred nature of water, in these stories recounted by three individuals, mermaids are seen as a version of a witch with power to do harm. These stories all involve the abduction of men who reside with mermaids in their homes under the sea. Those who have seen a mermaid differ on where they live. Some say it is in the Atlantic, some say it is close by the mouth of the Mississippi, while someone else saw a mermaid hole by the banks of the Alabama River.

I.

Before they had any steam, ships were sailed across the Atlantic. The Atlantic was fifteen miles deep, and there were mermaids in those days. And if you called anybody's name on the ship, they would ask for it, "Give it to me." And if you didn't give it to them they would capsize the ship.

So, the captain had to change the men's names to different objects—hatchet, ax, hammer, furniture. Whenever he wanted a man to do something, he'd call to him, "Hammer, go on deck and look out." The mermaid would holler, "Give me hammer." So, they threw the hammer overboard to her, and the vessel would proceed on. The captain might say, "Ax, you go on down in the kindling room start a fire in the boiler; it's going dead." Then the mermaid said, "Give me ax." So, they had to throw her an iron ax. Next day he says, "Chair, go down in the stateroom and make up those beds." And the mermaid yells, "Give me chair." So, they had to throw a whole suite of furniture overboard.

One day he made a mistake and forgot and said, "Sam, go in the kitchen and cook supper." The mermaid right away calls, "Give me Sam." They didn't have anything on the ship that was named Sam, so they had to throw Sam overboard. Soon as Sam hit the water, she grabbed him. Her hair was so long she could wrap him up—he didn't even get wet. And she was swimming so fast he could catch breath under the water. When she got home and unwrapped Sam out of her hair, she said, "Oooh, you sure do look nice. Do you like fish?"

Sam said, "No, I won't even cook a fish."

"Well, we'll get married," she replied. And so, they were married.

After a while Sam began to step out with other mermaids. His girlfriend became jealous of him and his wife, and they had a fight over Sam. The wife whipped her, and told her, "You can't see Sam never again."

The girlfriend said, "I'll get even with you."

One day Sam's girlfriend asked him if he wanted to go back to his native home. He said yes. So, she grabbed him, wrapped him in her hair, and swum with the same fastness as his wife did when she was carrying him, so he could catch breath. When she got to land, she put him onto the ground on the bank. "Now if he can't do me no good, he sure won't do her none," she said. That was Sam's experience in the mermaid's home in the bottom of the sea.

Then he told the others how nice her home was, all fixed up with the furniture and other things. There weren't any men down there—guess that's why they ain't any mermaids anymore. Sam said they had purple lips, just like women are painted today. You see pictures of mermaids with lips like that. In old days people didn't wear lipstick, and I think they got the idea from seeing those pictures.

Sam told the people the mermaid's house was built like the alligator's. He digs in the bank at water level; then he goes up—nature teaches him how high to go—then digs down to water level again, and there he makes his home, in rooms ten to twenty feet long. The mermaid builds in the wall of the sea like the alligator. Sam stayed down there six years. If he hadn't got to co'ting he'd a still be there, I guess.

II.

My mother told us about the mermaid. If it's a story somebody was putting it out, we...well, we believed it as the truth.

The mermaids had different booths they stayed in. They'd go out and meet the ship and call for people by name. This one mermaid called for Aleck, who was a colored man. The sailors knew that Aleck's time was coming, or that she'd wreck the ship. So, they threw Aleck out, and she put her hair right over his face and took him to her little booth. And she had everything in there he wanted to eat—beef and fruits. And she had rocks fixed for him to cook on even though she ate everything raw. She combed her hair all day and sang.

The water passed by and never came in. She'd set up on the bank and her tail was in the water. It was a blindfold of water. There was a bank for him to sit on. Every day she would ask him, "Aleck, do you like fish?"

And he would say, "No." They teach you to say that on the ships.

Sailors know that if mermaids don't bring the man back in six months, she done killed him. At the end of six months she says, "Aleck, your ship is coming." And she'd picked him up and carry him on up and asked for another one. And she'd ask for flour and meat, just as plain.

I don't see why they don't hear 'em now, or how they don't get those little raft boats after 'em. Maybe they do. Funny there was no men there, just women.

Mother seen Aleck. He lived in Aberdeen, Mississippi. I seen a mermaid in Ringling Brothers Show.

III.

Place not far from my hometown, on the riverbank—the Alabama River—they used to see the mermaid. When the boats were running on the Alabama River, steamboats would bring up groceries from Mobile to the farmers: caraway syrup, flour, sugar, and rice. The boat came up to the wharf, and a fellow on the boat working there, a cabin boy, saw the mermaid out in the water and laughed at her. From her navel up is a lady, down is a fish tail. She had long hair.

He was on the platform carrying the groceries to the wharf, and she slapped him with her tail and knocked him into the water. Then she took her hair and wrapped his face in it, so he wouldn't get drowned, and took him about half a mile downstream to her mermaid home. He stayed there eight or nine years. People claim he got sick down there. Everything they gave him he just vomit, vomit. So, they took him up to the land, wrapped in their hair, and left him on the bank. Then the mermaid rise up in the water, to see if he was sick on land. But the mermaid couldn't follow him, 'cause she was to walk on her hands.

The people didn't know him 'cause he was so hairy. He didn't have on no clothes. But he knew them. He shaved up and got natural; he favored himself. But he looked like some kind of animal before. He nearly died in that desert down there.

I knew where that mermaid hole was. They had pretty stools for them to sit on. It's a place about as big as the gable end of this house, but you can't see it because it's dark as midnight. It's by the bank, and they lay their backs on the stools, and play around, and when they see people come, they slide down into the water. It's the best kind of water, spring water.

You can paddle your skiff boat right into the hole; the water runs into the hole. But everybody's afraid to go in.

Braziel Robinson and the Root-Doctors

Root-doctors practice medicine, often referred to as Hoodoo, conjuring, or having mojo. Known as Hoodoo priests or priestesses, conjurers, or conjure doctors, they have the additional power of seeing into the future. In African American folklore, being born with a caul or veil over one's face is a symbol of having these spiritual powers. Root-doctors can manufacture charms, gris-gris bags, and conjure bottles, and produce various other items of protection or harm. When a root-doctor uses his or her power to harm someone, only another more powerful root-doctor can break the spell. The importance of Hoodoo cannot be understated, especially in the nineteenth and twentieth centuries, although it was practiced during slavery and is still performed today, especially in the southern United States. Conjuring cures illnesses, provides protection, and generally grants redress in an often-hostile world dominated by whites. Conjuring came from African spiritual beliefs and mixed with European and Native American medicine. It even incorporated the Bible. Some scholars claim conjuring is the most important African feature of the Black community that survived slavery. This story is about Braziel Robinson, a man emancipated after the Civil War, who explains conjuring.

People born with a caul generally live to be old. The caul is always buried in a graveyard.

Children born with a caul talk sooner than other children, and have lot more sense.

I was conjured in May 1898, while hoeing cotton. I took off my shoes and hoed two rows, then I felt strange; my feet begun to swell, and then my legs, and then, I couldn't walk. I had to stop and go home. Just as I stepped in the house, I felt the terriblest pain in my jints. I sat down and thought, and then looked in my shoes. I found some yaller dirt, and knew it was graveyard dirt—then I knew I was conjured. I then hunted about to find if there was any conjure in the house and found a bag under my door-step. I opened the bag and found, some small roots about an inch long, some black hair, a piece of snake skin, and some graveyard dirt, dark-yaller, right off some coffin. I took the bag and dug a hole in the public road in front of my house, and buried it with the dirt out of my shoes, and throwed some red pepper all around the house. I didn't get any better, and went and saw a root-doctor, who told me he could take off the conjure. He gave me a cup of tea to drink and mixed up something and put it in a jug to wash my feet and legs with, but it ain't done me much good; he ain't got enough power. I am gwine to see one in Augusta, who has great power, and can tell me who conjured me. They say root-doctors have power over spirits, who will tell them who does the conjuring; they ginerally uses yerbs gathered on the changes of the moon, and must be got at night. People git conjur from the root-doctors and one root-doctor often works against another, the one that has the most power does the work.

<182>

People gits most conjured by giving them snake's heads, lizards, and scorpions, dried and beat up into powder and putting it in the food or water they drink, and then they gits full of the varmints; I saw a root-doctor cut out of a man's leg a lizard and a grasshopper, and then he got well. Some conjur ain't to kill, but to make a person sick or make him have pain, and then conjur is put on the ground in the path where the person to be conjured goes. It is put down on a young moon, a growing moon, so the conjur will rise up and grow, so the person stepping over it will git conjured. Sometimes they roll it up in a ball and tie it to a string and hang it from a limb, so the person to be conjured, coming by, touches the ball, and the work's done, and he gits conjured in the part that strikes the ball. The ball is small and tied by a thread so a person can't see it. There are many ways to conjur, I knew a man that was conjured by putting graveyard dirt under his house in small piles and it almost killed him, and his wife. The dirt made holes in the ground, for it will always go back as deep as you got it, it goes down to where it naturally belongs.

Only root-doctors can git the graveyard dirt; they know what kind to git and when. The hants won't let everybody git it, they must git it thro' some kind of spell, for the graveyard dirt works trouble 'til it gits back inter the ground, and then wears off. It must git down to the same depth it was took from, that is as deep as the coffin lid was from the surface of the ground.

The Flying Man

Often referred to as "The Flying African," this legend is rooted in the islands off the South Carolina and Georgia coasts. Commonly spoken among the Gullah people, it claims a group of enslaved African people used magic to escape bondage and return to their home in Africa by flight. Some tellers claim they went in groups while chanting. Others say they flew "like a bird" and that bird was a buzzard. All variations of this tale say the flight took the enslaved back to their homeland. Stories filled with hope and promise helped enslaved people reconcile their current situations against the idea that one day, they could be free. And so these hopeful tales spread far and wide and sightings of flyings Africans were reported across the country.

I heard about the flying man up in Arkansas, at Jonesboro. The polices went up to him, and the faster they walked the faster he walked, until he just spread his arms and sailed right off. And they never did catch him. Said he was faster than the planes. They told about him all through the South, in Alabama, Mississippi, Arkansas.

Permissions

All stories are public domain unless otherwise noted. Licensed content used with permission.

The Ballad of John Henry

Bell, Arthur. "John Henry." John and Ruby Lomax 1939 Southern States Recording Trip (AFC1939/001). Cummins State Farm in Gould, Arkansas. May 20, 1939. sound disc : analog, 78 rpm ; 12 in. American Folklife Center, Library of Congress. MP3. https://www.loc.gov/item/lomaxbib000326/.

Why Men and Women Don't Have Tails Like Cows

How the Gopher Turtle Was Made

Uncle Monday

Railroad Bill

Diddy-Wah-Diddy

Big John Gives Old Master a Sign

A Ghost Story About an Aunt

Condon, Kristin G. Uncle Monday and Other Florida Tales. Jackson, MS: University of Mississippi Press, 2001.

The Tar Baby

Dividing Souls

The Yearling

Big Feet Contest

The Fight

The Swimming Contest

How a Hoodoo Doctor Works

Dorson, Richard M. American Negro Folktales. Greenwich, CT: Fawcett Publications, 1956.

Ógún and Aerosol Art

Miller, Ivor L. Aerosol Kingdom: Subway Painters of New York City. Jackson, MS: University of Mississippi Press, 2002.

Resources

Abdurraqib, Hanif. *A Little Devil in America: Notes in Praise of Black Performance.* New York,

NY: Random House, 2021.

Alexander, Elizabeth. *The Trayvon Generation.* New York, NY: Grand Central Publishing, 2022.

Als, Hilton. *White Girls.* San Francisco, CA: McSweeny's, 2014.

Anderson, Carol. Foreword by Dick Durbin. *One Person, No Vote: How Voter Suppression is Destroying Our Democracy.* New York, NY: Bloomsbury Publishing, 2018.

Axelrod, Alan, and Harry Oster. *The Penguin Dictionary of American Folklore.* New York, NY: Penguin Putnam, 2000.

Bettelheim, Bruno. *The Uses of Enchantment: The Meaning and Importance of Fairy Tales.* New York, NY: Vintage Books, 1977.

Boyd, Valerie. *Wrapped in Rainbows: The Life of Zora Neale Hurston.* New York, NY: Scribner, 2003.

Brown, Mary Ellen, and Bruce A. Rosenberg (Eds.) *Encyclopedia of Folklore and Literature.* Santa Barbara, CA: ABC-Clio, 1998.

Coats, Ta-Nehisi. *Between the World and Me.* New York, NY: Spiegel & Grau, 2015.

Commander, Michelle D. (Introduction by Ian Alteveer, Hannah Beachler, and Sarah Lawrence.)*Before Yesterday We Could Fly: An Afrofuturist Period Room.* New York, NY: The Metropolitan Museum of Art, 2022.

Cone, James H. *The Cross and the Lynching Tree.* Maryknoll, NY: Orbis Books, 2011.

Crafts, Hannah. (Edited by Henry Louis Gates, Jr.) *The Bondwoman's Narrative.* New York, NY: Grand Central Publishing, 2003.

Du Bois, W. E. B. *The Souls of Black Folk*. New York, NY: Dover, 1994. (First published in1903).

Dyson, Michael Eric. *What Truth Sounds Like: Robert F. Kennedy, James Baldwin, and Our Unfinished Conversation About Race in America*. New York, NY: St. Martin's Press, 2018.

Dyson, Michael Eric. *Entertaining Race: Performing Blackness in America*. New York, NY: St. Martin's Press, 2021.

English, Darby & Charlotte Barat. (Forward by Glenn D. Lowry) *Among Others: Blackness at MoMA*. New York, NY: The Museum of Modern Art, 2019.

Fanon, Franz. (Foreword by Kwame Anthony Appiah in 2008.) *Black Skin, White Masks*. NewYork, NY: Grove, 1952.

Gates, Jr., Henry Louis. *Stony the Road: Reconstruction, White Supremacy, and the Rise of Jim Crow*. New York, NY: Penguin Press, 2019

Gates, Henry Louis, Jr. *The Signifying Monkey: A Theory of Afro-American Literary Criticism*. New York, NY: Oxford University Press, 1988.

Gates, Henry Louis, Jr. *The Black Church: This is Our Story, This is Our Song*. New York, NY: Penguin Press, 2021.

Garza, Alicia. *The Purpose of Power: How We Come Together When We Fall Apart*. New York, NY: One World, 2020.

Gordon, Linda. *The Second Coming of the KKK: The Ku Klux Klan of the 1920s and the American Political Tradition*. New York, NY: Liveright Publishing Corporation, 2017.

Green, Thomas A. *The Greenwood Library of American Folktales*. New York, NY: Bloomsbury Publishing, 2006.

Hannah-Jones, Nikole, Ilena Silverman & Jake Silverstein (Eds.) *The 1619 Project: A New Origin Story*. New York, NY: One World, 2021.

Haygood, Wil. *Colorization: One Hundred Years of Black Films in a White World*. New York, NY: Alfred A. Knopf, 2021.

Hurston, Zora Neale. (Edited by Deborah G. Plant.) *Barracoon: The Story of the Last "Black Cargo."* New York, NY: Amistad, 2018.

Ingram, Jessica. *Road Through Midnight: A Civil Rights Memorial*. Chapel Hill, NC: The University of North Carolina Press, 2020.

Isenberg, Nancy. *White Trash: The 400-Year Untold History of Class in America*. New York, NY: Penguin Books, 2016.

Ivey, Bill. *Building an Enlightened World: Folklorizing America*. Bloomington, IN: Indiana University Press, 2018.

Jacobs, Harriet A. (Jean Fagan Yellin, Ed.) *Incidents in the Life of a Slave Girl: Written by Herself*. Cambridge, MA: Harvard University Press, 1987.

Jones, Robert P. *White Too Long: The Legacy of White Supremacy in American Christianity*. New York, NY: Simon & Schuster, 2020.

Kendi, Abram X. *How to Be an Antiracist*. New York, NY: One World, 2019.

Lemon, Don. *This Is the Fire: What I Say to My Friends About Racism*. New York, NY: Little, Brown and Company, 2021.

McDonough, Gary W., (Ed.) *The Florida Negro: A Federal Writers' Project Legacy*. Jackson. MS: University Press of Mississippi, 1993.

McGhee, Heather. *The Sum of Us: What Racism Costs Everyone and How We Can Prosper Together*. New York, NY: One World, 2021.

Mills, Kay. (Forward by Marian Wright Edelman.) *This Little Light of Mine: The Life of Fannie Lou Hamer*. Lexington, KY: The University Press of Kentucky, 2007.

Oliver, Valerie Cassel Olive. *The Dirty South: Contemporary Art, Material Culture, and the Sonic Impulse.* Richmond, VA: Virginia Museum of Fine Arts and Duke University Press, 2021.

Oluo, Ijeoma.*So You Want to Talk About Race.* New York, NY: Seal Press, 2018.

Pedrosa, Adriano & Tomas Toledo. (Eds.) *Afro-Atlantic Histories.* New York, NY: DelMonico Books, 2022.

Perry, Imani. *Breathe: A Letter to My Sons.* Boston, MA: Beacon Press, 2019.

Perry, Imani. *South to America: A Journey Below the Mason-Dixon to Understanding the Soul of a Nation.* New York, NY: Harper Collins, 2022.

Puckett, Newbell Niles. *Folk Beliefs of the Southern Negro.* Delhi, India: Alpha Editions, 2020.

Rembert, Winfred as told to Erin I. Kelly. (Forward by Bryan Stevenson.) *Chasing Me to My Grave: An Artist's Memoir of the Jim Crow South.* New York, NY: Bloomsbury, 2021.

Renal, Margaret. *Graceland at Last: Notes on Hope and Heartache from the American South.* Minneapolis, MN: Milkweed, 2021.

Tell, Dave. *Remembering Emmett Till.* Chicago, IL: The University of Chicago Press, 2019.

Thompson, Robert. Ferris. *Flash of the Spirit.* New York, NY: Vintage, 2010.

Thompson, Robert Ferris. *Face of the Gods: Art and Altars of African and the African Americas.* New York, NY: Prestel, 1993

White, Walter. (Introduction by Kenneth Robert Jansen.) *Rope and Faggot: A Biography of Judge Lynch.* Notre Dame, IN: Alfred A Knopf, Inc., 1929 (2001).

Wilderson III, Frank B. *Afropessimism*. New York, NY: Liveright Publishing Corporation, 2020.

Wilkerson, Isabel. *Caste: The Origins of Our Discontents*. New York, NY: Random House, 2020.

Wilson, Charles Reagan, and William Ferris, (Eds.) *Encyclopedia of Southern Culture*.

Chapel Hill, NC: The University of North Carolina Press, 1980.

Wood, Amy Louise. *Lynching and Spectacle: Witnessing Racial Violence in America, 1890–1940*. Chapel Hill, NC: The University of North Carolina Press, 2009.

Index

First published in 2025 by Wellfleet Press, an imprint of The Quarto
Group,142 West 36th Street, 4th Floor, New York, NY 10018, USA
(212) 779-4972 www.Quarto.com

Wellfleet titles are also available at discount for retail, wholesale,
promotional, and bulk purchase. For details, contact the Special Sales
Manager by email at specialsales@quarto.com or by mail at The Quarto
Group, Attn: Special Sales Manager, 100 Cummings Center Suite 265D,
Beverly, MA 01915 USA.

10 9 8 7 6 5 4 3 2 1

ISBN: 978-1-57715-516-4

Digital edition published in 2025
eISBN: 978-0-7603-9535-6

Library of Congress Control Number: 2024945276

Group Publisher: Rage Kindelsperger
Editorial Director: Erin Canning
Creative Director: Laura Drew
Managing Editor: Cara Donaldson
Editorial Assistant: Alyana Nurani
Introductions: Kristin G. Congdon
Cover Design: Marisa Kwek
Interior Design: Raine Rath
Collage Artist: Mirlande Jean-Gilles

Printed in China

This book provides general information on various widely known and widely accepted images that tend to evoke feelings of strength and confidence. However, it should not be relied upon as recommending or promoting any specific diagnosis or method of treatment for a particular condition, and it is not intended as a substitute for medical or mental health advice or for direct diagnosis and treatment of a medical or mental health condition by a qualified physician. Readers who have questions about a particular condition, possible treatments for that condition, or possible reactions from the condition or its treatment should consult a physician or other qualified health care professional.

The Quarto Group denounces any and all forms of hate, discrimination, and oppression and does not condone the use of its products in any practices aimed at harming or demeaning any group or individual.

Editor's Note: Out of respect for the storytellers who originally shared these tales, we have elected in most cases to retain the dialect of the people at a certain time in history. However, in some instances where certain words could be misleading, we corrected the spelling. Additionally, while we have chosen to use more contemporary language around slavery in our explanatory text, we have retained the originally chosen words of these stories to maintain authenticity. The same goes for how the storytellers chose to refer to themselves.